A Study of
The Angelic Realm

Angelology, Satanology, and Demonology

Other Books by Dr. Arnold G. Fruchtenbaum

A Passover Haggadah for Jewish Believers

An Historical and Geographical Study Guide of Israel: With a Supplement on Jordan

Ariel's Harmony of the Gospels

Faith Alone: The Condition of Our Salvation (An Exposition of the Book of Galatians and Other Relevant Topics)

God's Will & Man's Will: Predestination, Election, and Free Will

Ha-Mashiach: The Messiah of the Hebrew Scriptures

Israelology: The Missing Link in Systematic Theology

Jesus Was a Jew

The Feasts and Fasts of Israel – Their Historic and Prophetic Significance

The Footsteps of the Messiah: A Study of the Sequence of Prophetic Events

The Historical and Geographical Maps of Israel and Surrounding Territories

The Remnant of Israel: The History, Theology, and Philosophy of the Messianic Jewish Community

The Sabbath

What the Bible Teaches About Israel: Past, Present, and Future (An Abridged Version of Israelology: The Missing Link in Systematic Theology)

Yeshua: The Life of Messiah from a Messianic Jewish Perspective, Volumes 1-4 & The Abridged Version

Ariel's Bible Commentary Series:

Biblical Lovemaking: A Study of the Song of Solomon

Judges and Ruth

The Book of Acts

The Book of Genesis

The Messianic Jewish Epistles (Hebrews, James, I & II Peter, Jude)

Ariel's Come and See Series:

The Word of God: Its Nature and Content

What We Know About God: Theology Proper

Messiah Yeshua, Divine Redeemer: Christology from a Messianic Jewish Perspective

Ruach HaKodesh – God the Holy Spirit: Messianic Jewish Perspectives on Pneumatology

A STUDY OF
THE ANGELIC REALM

ANGELOLOGY, SATANOLOGY, AND
DEMONOLOGY

ARNOLD G. FRUCHTENBAUM
TH.M., PH.D.

A Study of the Angelic Realm
Angelology, Satanology, and Demonology
(Arnold G. Fruchtenbaum, Th.M., Ph.D.)
Volume 5 in Ariel's "Come and See" Series
1ˢᵗ Edition © 2020 by Ariel Ministries

ISBN 978-1-951059-68-2

Library of Congress Control Number: 2020920174
REL101000 RELIGION / Messianic Judaism / Angels / Demons / Satan

Editor: Christiane K. Jurik, M.A.
Cover illustration by Jesse and Josh Gonzales

We thank our team of proofreaders—including Pauline Ilsen, Udaya Thangasamy, Valerie Clearly, Laurie Combs, Sharon Phinney—for their work.

All Scripture quotations, unless otherwise noted, are from the *1901 American Standard Version* (Oak Harbor, WA: Logos Research Systems, Inc., 1994). However, the archaic language has been changed with one exception: The archaic *ye* has been retained to distinguish the second-person plural from the singular *you*. The words "Jesus" and "Christ" have been replaced with "Yeshua" and "Messiah."

Printed in the United States of America

Published by Ariel Ministries
P.O. Box 792507
San Antonio, TX 78279-2507
www.ariel.org

This volume is dedicated in memory of

Dr. Ralph Beich

Who taught me Biblical Hebrew and Koine Greek

at Shelton College.

Contents

Preface

What is Come and See?

Come and See is a multi-volume collection of Messianic Bible studies transcribed from Dr. Arnold Fruchtenbaum's original radio broadcasts. For the book series, the manuscripts made from these transcripts were edited and expanded, and text based on his sermon notes was added.

Each study is a solid foundation upon which you can stand—a whiteboard from which you can teach or a podium from which you can preach the uncompromised truth to your congregation. This extensive collection is replete with expert knowledge of Hebrew, Greek, the Talmud, the history of the Jews, the geography of *Eretz Yisrael* (the land of Israel); a scholar's command of the Word; and the illumination of the *Ruach HaKodesh* (the Holy Spirit). *Come and See* will edify you in your personal devotion or small group Bible study regardless of which topic you choose.

What Will You Discover in This Volume?

Volume five of *Come and See* examines an area of systematic theology called "angelology." Literally, this term means "the doctrine of angels." Because there are fallen and unfallen angels, the topic will be discussed in three parts. The first part covers angelology proper, meaning the doctrine of unfallen angels. The second part deals with Satanology, which is the doctrine of Satan. The third part covers demonology, which is the doctrine of fallen angels.

Systematic theology is, of course, a logical development of what the Bible teaches about various subjects. The first main division is bibliology, which is the study of the Scriptures. We addressed the topic in volume one of *Come and See*, titled *The Word of God*. This is a logical beginning, since what we know about theology comes from the Scriptures themselves.

The second main division of systematic theology is theology proper, which is the doctrine of God. We addressed this topic in volume two of this series, titled *What We Know About God*. The study developed our understanding of God the Father and emphasized the deity, the theism, and the trinitarianism of God.

The third main division of systematic theology is Christology, also called "the doctrine of the Son" or "the doctrine of the Messiah." We covered this topic in volume three of our *Come and See* series, titled *Messiah Yeshua, Divine Redeemer: Christology from a Messianic Jewish Perspective*.

The fourth main division of systematic theology is pneumatology, also called "the doctrine of the Holy Spirit." We covered this topic in volume four of our *Come and See* series, titled *Ruach HaKodesh God the Holy Spirit: Messianic Jewish Perspectives on Pneumatology*.

Questions and Study Suggestions for the Course

At the end of each chapter, you will find questions and study suggestions which provide application that is relevant to the subject.

The goal of this collection is for disciples of *Yeshua* (Jesus) to grow in their faith and to live out their calling to make disciples. We hope you enjoy the *Come and See Series*!

Part 1:

Angelology Proper

Chapter I

God's Heavenly Host

Angelology proper deals with what the Bible teaches about good angels, those who did not fall with Satan.

Elect or unfallen angels are given two specific titles in Scripture. They are called "elect angels" and "holy angels." These titles are based on three verses. First, in I Timothy 5:21, unfallen angels are called *elect angels*, which means they were elected not to fall and have been confirmed in their holiness. After God created Adam and Eve, He subjected them to a test in the garden of Eden to see if they would be obedient or disobedient. In the same way, after God created the angels, He then subjected them to a test to see if they would be obedient or disobedient. One-third of the angels chose to be disobedient to God and followed Satan in his fall; those angels became demons. But two-thirds of the angels chose not to follow Satan, and therefore they were confirmed in their holiness. Confirmed holiness means that the period of testing and probation is over, and the created beings are no longer capable of sinning. When believers receive their resurrection bodies, they will also be confirmed in their holiness, and in their resurrection bodies, they too will not be capable of sinning. God Himself has always been confirmed in His holiness; He is incapable of sinning. Because the unfallen angels are no longer capable of sinning, they are called "elect angels."

The second title for unfallen angels is "holy angels." It is found in Mark 8:38 and Luke 9:26. Unfallen angels are called "holy" as opposed to fallen angels, who are wicked and unholy.

A. Wrong Views

There are a number of wrong views regarding angels. For instance, it has been taught that angels are merely transient emanations or temporary "forces" from God. The term "emanation" refers to the emergence of all things from the unchanging and perfect God. Neoplatonists used the term to describe God's creation of the universe as something automatic and unwilled, like a body's production of a shadow.[1] In this view, all reality consists of a series of emanations from God, who is the eternal source of this cosmic process. If angels were emanations from God, it would mean that they were not created willfully. Gnostics have claimed that angels are permanent emanations (*aeons*) from God.[2]

It has also been taught that angels are glorified human beings; that is, when a believer dies and goes to heaven, he becomes an angel.

Among unbelievers, a common teaching is that angels do not exist. They believe that Yeshua mentioned angels just to accommodate Himself to the popular thinking of His day, but that He Himself knew better.

B. The Existence of Angels

In the Scriptures, there are 273 references to angels in 33 of the 66 books. This means that half of all books of the Bible mention angels.

---

[1] Neoplatonism is based on the general ideas of Platonism. It strives to understand the world on the basis of a single cause that is divine. It teaches that existence is defined by thought and intellect, not matter. Neoplatonic philosophy emerged in the second century A.D. and influenced Christian theology throughout the Late Antiquity and the Middle Ages, especially because scholars such as Origen (ca. A.D. 184-253) and Augustine of Hippo (A.D. 354-430) adopted its principles into their theologies.

[2] Gnosticism is a philosophy that claims salvation is dependent on divine knowledge. Only those who have obtained such higher knowledge are freed from the deceptions of evil. The doctrine is based on two false assumptions. First, it teaches that matter is evil and spirit is good. Real life exists in the spirit realm only. Consequently, any sin done in the body is inconsequential. Second, only a few privileged people possess divine or saving knowledge. They acquired this higher knowledge on a level of existence that supersedes all other levels. Therefore, those who possess this higher knowledge are elevated above everyone else.

In the Hebrew Scriptures, angels are mentioned 108 times in 18 books: Genesis, Exodus, Numbers, Judges, I and II Samuel, I and II Kings, I and II Chronicles, Job, Psalms, Ecclesiastes, Isaiah, Ezekiel, Daniel, Hosea, and Zechariah. It should be noted that angels are not only mentioned in the apocalyptical books of the Old Testament, but also in the prophetic, historical, and poetic books.

In the New Testament, angels are mentioned a total of 165 times in 15 books: Matthew, Mark, Luke, John, Acts, Romans, II Corinthians, Galatians, Colossians, II Thessalonians, I Timothy, I and II Peter, Jude, and Revelation. As with the Hebrew Scriptures, all types of New Testament literature mention the existence of angels.

Considering the above information, it is obvious that Scripture clearly teaches the existence of angels from the first book, Genesis, to the last book, Revelation. Angels are not only mentioned in the earlier books, but also in the later books; the mention of angels is scattered throughout the Scriptures. In other words, the mention of angels is not peculiar to just one author, nor is it peculiar to visionary authors.

Furthermore, Yeshua Himself clearly taught the existence of angels and referred to them in every Gospel:

- ✿ Matthew 13:39, 41, 49; 16:27; 18:10; 22:30; 24:31, 36; 25:31; 26:53
- ✿ Mark 8:38; 12:25; 13:32
- ✿ Luke 9:26; 12:8-9; 15:10; 16:22; 20:36
- ✿ John 1:51

In light of the Messiah's teaching on the existence of angels, there are five options to evaluate. The first option is that Yeshua was deceived. He taught the existence of angels and believed in the existence of angels even though angels do not really exist. This, of course, would mean that He was deceived.

The second option is that Yeshua was being deceptive. While He Himself did not believe in angels and knew that angels do not exist, He was merely being deceptive when He spoke about them.

The third option is that Yeshua was not trying to be deceptive, but was simply accommodating His teachings to the common beliefs of that day so the people would understand the main truths of what He was saying. Perhaps this view seems a little better than saying Yeshua was being deceptive, but actually, it is simply an attempt to be more euphemistic and ultimately means the same thing.

The fourth option is that Yeshua never mentioned the existence of angels nor did He teach the existence of angels; the writers of the Gospels put those words into His mouth. Therefore, it was not Yeshua who was being deceptive, but the writers of the Gospels. But if the Gospels cannot be trusted when they quote Yeshua on angels, how can they be trusted when they quote Him on anything?

The only valid option is the fifth option: Yeshua really did believe in the existence of angels and, therefore, taught their existence—because angels do exist.

C. Terms Used of Angels

When speaking about angels, the Scriptures use several words. Some of them describe the nature (what the celestial beings are or are like), some the status (the rank in the hierarchical order of God's heavenly host), and some the function (what the celestial beings do).

The first and most common term is "angel." In Hebrew, the word is *mal'âk* (*malak*) and in Greek, it is *ággelos*. Phonetically, this term could be spelled *angelos*, and it serves as the basis for the English word "angel." Both *mal'âk* and *ággelos* mean "messenger." Furthermore, in the biblical text, the same words are used of both human messengers and divine messengers. For example, a plural form of *mal'âk* is used of divine messengers in Genesis 32:1 and of human messengers in Genesis 32:3. Most Bible translations use two different words for this one Hebrew term. In dealing with the divine messenger, *mal'âk*, *ággelos*, and even the English translation "angel" are used as general terms for all celestial beings, be they actual angels, seraphs, or cherubs. Furthermore, the term is primarily, but not exclusively, a reference to the lowest order of celestial beings. The terms *mal'âk* and *ággelos* emphasize both office and function. In Hebrews 1:7, for example, it says: *And of the angels he says, Who makes his angels winds, And his ministers a flame a fire.* The term *ággelos* describes both the office and the function of angels in this verse. The office is that of a messenger, and the function is that of service.

A second term is "sons of God." This is strictly an Old Testament name. The Hebrew term, *bənê 'ĕlōhîm* (*benei elohim*) emphasizes the fact that angels were directly created by God. In the Old Testament, this term is always plural, and it always refers to angels. It is found in Genesis 6:2, 4; Job 1:6; and 2:1.

A third term is "sons of the Mighty." In Hebrew, the expression is *bənê 'ĕlîm* (*benei elim*). The title is similar to "sons of God," because God is the Mighty One. The term is found in Psalm 29:1 and 89:6. It again emphasizes that angels were directly created by God.

A fourth term is "the holy ones." In Hebrew, the expression is *qəḏōšîm* (*qadoshim*), and in Aramaic, it is *qaddîšîn* (*qaddishin*). This name emphasizes the state of unfallen angels and sets them apart from those celestial beings who fell and became demons. The term is found in verses such as Psalm 89:5, 7; Daniel 4:13 (in the Aramaic singular as *qaddîš* or *qaddish*), 17; and 8:13 (in Hebrew singular as *qāḏōwōš* or *qadosh*, meaning "sacred" and "holy").

A fifth term is "watcher," which emphasizes the function of observing. In the Scriptures, this term appears as *'îr* or *ir* (plural: *'îrîn* or *irin*), which is an Aramaic word meaning "waking or wakeful one." Angels observe whether God's will is being carried out. This name is found in Daniel 4:13, 17, and 23.

The sixth term is "watchmen," which is *šōmərîm* (*shomerim*) in Hebrew. This name also emphasizes the function of observation. While "watcher" emphasizes purely the aspect of observation to see if God's will is being carried out, the term "watchmen" also carries the concept of guarding. Angels are guardians watching over a situation. An example of this usage is found in Isaiah 62:6.

The seventh term is "spirits," for angels are spirit beings. In the New Testament, the Greek word for "spirit" is *pneuma*. The plural, *pneumata*, is used, for example, in Hebrews 1:14.

The eighth name is "stars." With very few exceptions (such as Numbers 24:17), whenever the word "star" is used symbolically in the Scriptures, it is always a symbol for angels. In Hebrew, the term is *kôḵāḇ* (*kokab*, singular) or *kôḵâḇîm* (*kokabim*, plural), found in passages such as Job 38:7. In Greek, the term is *astēr* (singular) or *asterōn* (plural), found in Revelation 1:20; 9:1; and 12:4.

A ninth term is "ministers." It emphasizes the fact that angels are ministers of God, carrying out His will. The Hebrew term for "ministers" is *məšârəṯâw* (*meshartav*) from the verb *šâraṯ* (*sharat*), "to minister." It is found in Psalm 103:21 and 104:4. The Greek term, *leitourgos*, is used in Hebrews 1:7.

A tenth name for angels is "host." The Hebrew word for "host" is *ṣâḇâʾ* (*tsaba*) in the singular and *ṣâḇâʾōṯ* (*tsebaoth*) in the plural. Literally, it means "army." The host comprises the heavenly army of God. This is why God is often referred to as Jehovah of hosts or the Lord of hosts, for He is the Lord of this angelic army. The term is seen in I Kings 22:19; Psalm 103:20-21; and 148:2.

An eleventh term for angels is "chariots," emphasizing their speed in carrying out the will of the Lord. The Hebrew word for "chariots," *reḵeḇ* (*rekeb*), is found in II Kings 6:17 and Psalm 68:17. The synonym, *merkâḇâ* (*merkabah*), is used in Zechariah 6:1-8.

The twelfth term for angels is "gods." The Hebrew word for "gods" is *ʾĕlōhîm* (*elohim*). It is used of the one true God and the many false gods. It is also used of angels because angels are the representatives of God and have God's delegated authority to speak in His name. Because they speak authoritatively in God's name, they are referred to as *ʾĕlōhîm*. This is seen by comparing Psalm 8:5 with Hebrews 2:7:

- ✡ Psalm 8:5: *For you have made him but little lower than God [ʾĕlōhîm], And crown him with glory and honor.*
- ✡ Hebrews 2:7: *You made him a little lower than the angels [angelous]; You crowned him with glory and honor, And did set him over the works of your hands.*

D. The Creation of Angels

Angels are created beings. This fact is taught in Colossians 1:16, which states: *In him were all things created, in the heavens and upon the earth, things visible and things invisible, whether thrones or dominions or principalities or powers; all things have been created through him, and unto him.* The main point of this verse is that everything was created. But there is a special emphasis on the angelic beings, because the verse speaks about "things in the heavens." This phrase would include angels. The verse also mentions "things invisible." Again, this phrase would include angels. Then, the verse lists "thrones," "dominions," "principalities," and "powers." As will be seen later in this chapter, these terms describe the different ranks of angelic beings. The verse makes three additional points. First, God did not create some angels at one point and more angels at another point. Rather, all angels were created simultaneously. Second, the number of angels does not increase, as God is not continually creating new angels. Third, the number of angels also does not decrease, as once they were created, angels exist forever; they cannot be destroyed.

Since angels are created beings, they did not always exist. However, according to Job 38:4-7, they were already in existence when God created the heavens and the earth in Genesis 1:1. So, angels were created prior to the creation of the material universe. Therefore, they also preceded man. It is not known how long before Genesis 1:1 they were created, but that, indeed, they were.

God created the angels as holy beings, with the power of contrary choice. This is taught in Mark 8:38 and Jude 6. The power of contrary choice means they had the ability to choose contrary to their nature. They had the ability to make an unholy choice, which one-third of them eventually did. The other two-thirds later became confirmed in their holiness and, therefore, could no longer choose to sin; they no longer have the power of contrary choice.

Two things should be noted concerning the position of angels. First, they are inferior to the Messiah as to His deity (Heb. 1:4-2:3) and in His humanity (Heb. 2:5-8). Second, they are superior to common man because they are higher beings than man. This is taught in Psalm 8:4-5; Hebrews 2:5-7; and II Peter 2:11.

E. The Number of Angels

There are several passages of Scripture that give hints concerning the number of angels.

- ✿ Deuteronomy 33:2: *ten thousands of holy ones*
- ✿ II Kings 6:17: *the mountain was full of horses and chariots* [rekeb] *of fire*
- ✿ Psalm 68:17: *The chariots* [rekeb] *of God are twenty thousand, even thousands upon thousands*
- ✿ Daniel 7:10: *thousands of thousands ministered unto him, and ten thousand times ten thousand stood before him*
- ✿ Matthew 26:53: *twelve legions of angels* (a legion consists of three thousand to six thousand soldiers)
- ✿ Luke 2:13: *a multitude of the heavenly host*
- ✿ Hebrews 12:22: *innumerable hosts of angels*
- ✿ Revelation 5:11: *ten thousand times ten thousand, and thousands of thousands*

How many angels are there? Myriads upon myriads. They are innumerable. Because of the concept of guardianship, there are at least as many angels as there are human beings on the face of the earth. This could also very well mean that there are as many angels as there are humans that will ever exist or that have existed, in combination or in totality.

F. The Abode, Sphere, and Appearance of Angels

In this point, three questions will be answered: Where do angels live? In which sphere do they operate? What is their appearance?

1. The Angelic Abode

According to Matthew 18:10, the angelic abode is heaven: *See that ye despise not one of these little ones: for I say unto you, that in heaven their angels do always behold the face of my Father who is in heaven.*

The following verses make the same point:

✧ Matthew 24:36: *the angels of heaven*

✧ Mark 12:25: *angels in heaven*

✧ Mark 13:32: *the angels in heaven*

✧ Luke 22:43: *an angel from heaven*

✧ Galatians 1:8: *an angel from heaven*

✧ II Thessalonians 1:7: *from heaven with the angels*

✧ Jude 6: Angels have a *proper habitation*

Throughout the Scriptures, angels are referred to as the hosts of heaven, and so, quite obviously, the angelic abode is heaven.

2. The Angelic Sphere

The term "angelic sphere" refers to the area of operation of celestial beings. While they live in heaven, they operate in two other spheres.

One sphere is called "the heavenly places" or "heavens." This can be seen from Ephesians 3:10, which mentions *the principalities and the powers in the heavenly places*. In Greek, the term for "heavenly places" is *epouraniois*, a word that, according to *Thayer's Greek Lexicon*, means "existing in or above heaven" and "heavenly."[3] In Ephesians 3:10, the term refers to the lower heavens, the heaven of the clouds, meaning "outer space."

The second sphere of operation is the earth. Angels are God's ministers to accomplish His will on the earth. As a result, they have special ministries and functions on earth. One example of their special powers on earth is seen in Revelation 8:1-2, which mentions *the seven angels that stand before God* in heaven. When these angels blow a trumpet, great physical things will happen on earth. Revelation 14:18 speaks of an angel who has power over fire. Revelation 16:5 speaks of an angel who has power over the waters. All of these verses show that the second sphere of angels is the earth.

---

[3] Accessed through https://biblehub.com/greek/2032.htm.

So, while angels do have a function in their abode in heaven, meaning the third heaven, their sphere is not limited to this place. They also operate in the sphere of outer space and in the sphere of the earth.

3. The Appearance of Angels

The Scriptures contain records of angels appearing to people. Sometimes, they appeared in a dream, as was true with Jacob in Genesis 28:12: *And he dreamed; and, behold, a ladder set up on the earth, and the top of it reached to heaven; and, behold, the angels of God ascending and descending on it.* Angels also appeared to humans in visions. Examples are Daniel (Dan. 10), Zechariah (Zech. 1:7-6:8), and John (Rev. 1:1; 21-22). Yet, a more common way angels became visible was by simple appearance. They suddenly manifested themselves, such as was the case at the tomb of Yeshua (Mt. 28:2-3; Mk. 16:5; Lk. 24:4; Jn. 20:12).

As to their form, angels always appeared as young men. This is seen in Genesis 18:1-2, 16, 22; 19:1-22; Mark 16:5; Luke 24:4; and Acts 1:10-11. Nowhere in the Scriptures do angels appear in the form of women, children, cupids, or old men.

The appearance of angels primarily had one effect: It caused fear. This is seen in Daniel 10:4-9; Matthew 28:2-6; Luke 1:11-12, 26-30; and 2:9.

G. The Personality of Angels

Some teach that angels are not personal beings, but that they are merely emanations, powers, or rays. The three main attributes of personality are intellect, emotion, and will. That which possesses all three attributes is a personality. If it can be shown that angels have these three attributes, it proves that they have personality.

Angels have intellect. II Samuel 14:20 speaks of *the wisdom of an angel.* To have wisdom certainly means to have intellect. Psalm 148:2 states that angels have the ability to praise, another characteristic that requires intellect. Matthew 24:36 notes that angels have the ability to know things. This, too, demands intellect. Matthew 28:5 speaks about the angels' ability to communicate, which again requires intellect. Ephesians 3:10 notes that they learn about God's manifold wisdom through the church. The fact that angels can learn something shows that they have intellect. Finally, I Peter 1:12 states that there are things angels desire to look into. Such a desire is the result of intellect.

Angels also have emotion. Job 38:7 and Luke 15:10 speak of angels experiencing joy. If they have joy, these beings must have emotion.

Finally, angels also have will. In Luke 2:13, they praise God, exercising their will. In Hebrews 1:6, they worship God. This is also an exercise of the will. Finally, according to Jude 6, some angels chose to leave their proper habitation, which was an exercise of will.

The Scriptures make it absolutely clear that angels have intellect, emotion, and will. Therefore, they are personalities and not mere emanations.

H. The Nature of Angels

There are four categories concerning the nature of angels: their creation, their bodies, their company, and their attributes.

1. The Creation of Angels

Colossians 1:16 states that angels are created beings. This point was brought out previously, but it was not mentioned what this means for their nature. Because angels are created beings, they have the limitations of "creaturehood." A created being is a creature, and a creature can never have all the powers, attributes, and abilities of the Creator. So, while angels are far superior to humans, they are greatly inferior to God.

For example, angels are not omnipresent, but are limited in space (Dan. 9:21-23; 10:10-14). Angels are not omnipotent, but are limited in strength, even though they are powerful and mighty (Dan. 10:10-14; II Pet. 2:11). For this reason, Michael the archangel needed divine assistance in Jude 9. Angels are not omniscient either, but are limited in knowledge. Matthew 24:36 states that they do not know when the Messiah is going to return. Ephesians 3:10 and I Peter 1:11-12 confirm the limitation in their knowledge, which is why angels continue learning. Someone who is omniscient has no need to learn anything; he knows all things.

2. The Bodies of Angels

Hebrews 1:14 calls angels "spirit beings," which means that they are immaterial. However, they do have some kind of corporeality and are not ghosts. Luke 24:39 points out that this corporeality does not consist of *flesh and bones*. Rather, the angelic body is composed of a spirit body. Nevertheless, angels can appear in bodily form (Gen. 18-19; Mt. 1:20; Lk. 1:11; Jn. 20:12; Heb. 13:2). Because angels are spirit beings and immaterial, they are generally not visible. But because they do have corporeality, they are able to appear in bodily form. As was previously mentioned, when angels appear in bodily form, they always appear as young men.

The angelic body is not limited to human concepts of space. According to Luke 8:30, a legion of angelic spirit bodies could exist in the very limited space of one man.

Another thing about the angelic body is that it does not reproduce after its kind. They are unable to marry and produce more angels. This is seen in Matthew 22:30 and Mark 12:25. However, this does not mean that angels are sexless beings. The Greek does have a neuter form, but does not use the neuter form for angels; it always uses the masculine noun *angelos* and the masculine pronouns that go with it. In Genesis 6, some fallen angels intermarried with human women and were thus able to produce a grotesque race. What they produced were not angels after their kind, since the angelic body is not reproducible.

3. The Company of Angels

Angels are a "company," not a race. This is seen in Hebrews 12:22: *But you have come to Mount Zion and to the city of the living God, the heavenly Jerusalem, to an innumerable company of angels* (NKJV). The concept of race implies the ability to reproduce after one's kind with particular racial characteristics. Since angels do not reproduce themselves, they are not considered a race, but a company. As a company, three things apply to them:

1. Angels are distinct from humans (Ps. 8:4-5).
2. They are higher beings than humans (Heb. 2:7; II Pet. 2:11).
3. Elect or good angels do not marry (Lk. 20:34-36).

4. The Attributes of Angels

Concerning the attributes of angels, four main features can be mentioned. First, angels are holy (Lk. 9:26). In their case, holiness means they are no longer capable of sinning. Because they have been confirmed in their holiness, angels cannot fall as they once could.

Second, angels are powerful and mighty. In this area, they are superior to any man who has ever lived. Psalm 103:20 speaks of angels as being mighty in strength. In Matthew 28:2, only one angel was needed to roll away the stone from the tomb of Yeshua; normally, several men would have been needed to move such a stone. One angel opened the prison doors in Acts 5:19. In Acts 12:7, an angel was able to snap off Peter's chains in prison. In Acts 12:23, an angel was able to smite Agrippa with a disease that would take his life. Angels are referred to by the term "powers" in Ephesians 1:21; 3:10; and Colossians 1:16. II Thessalonians 1:7 speaks of the angels of Yeshua's power, and II Peter 2:11 refers to the power of angels. So, the second key attribute of angels is power.

Third, unlike humans, angels are incapable of dying. Due to the nature of their creation, they have the attribute of immortality. This is seen in Luke 20:35-36.

Fourth, they are not divine. Therefore, it is forbidden to worship angels. This is seen in Colossians 2:18; Revelation 19:10; and 22:8-9.

I. The Organization of Angels

The Scriptures reveal the existence of a hierarchy among celestial beings. This can be seen in certain titles given to angels and in the order among angels.

1. Terms That Show Degrees of Organization

There are eight hierarchical terms that show categories and degrees of organization within the angelic realm.

The first term is "thrones." It is found in Colossians 1:16 in the context of all things created in Yeshua, both *in the heavens and upon the earth*. These things are visible and invisible, *whether thrones or dominions or principalities or powers*. The angels sitting on these thrones are in the immediate presence of God and are exercising authority.

The second term is "dominions." The word is found in Ephesians 1:21 and Colossians 1:16. It emphasizes the concept of rulership. Hence, this category of angels rules over a specific area, and their rulership includes higher angels ruling over lower angels.

A third term is "principalities." The word is again found in Ephesians 1:21 and Colossians 1:16. It emphasizes the concept of governing. While the term "dominions" concerns higher angels ruling over lower angels, principalities are angelic rulers of nations.

A fourth term is "authorities." The word appears in Ephesians 1:21 and I Peter 3:22 and means "to exercise supremacy."

The fifth term is "powers." It is found in Ephesians 1:21; 3:10; Colossians 1:16; and I Peter 3:22. The term emphasizes the concept of imperial responsibilities.

The sixth term is "hosts." As was pointed out before, the Hebrew word for "hosts" means "army." Hence, this title emphasizes the military organization of angels. It is found in I Samuel 1:11 and I Kings 22:19.

A seventh term is "legions." It is found in Matthew 26:53. While the term "hosts" emphasizes the military organization as a whole, the word "legion" is one division within the host. One legion consists of up to 6,000 angels.

The eighth term is "chief prince" or "great prince." It is found in Daniel 10:13 and 12:1, where the chief prince is an angel who rules over a nation. [4]

2. The Order of Celestial Beings

While the terms given to angels indicate that there are a rank and an order among these beings, they do not reveal what this hierarchy looks like.

---

[4] For a full explanation of the historical and theological background of all of these terms, see: John B. Lightfoot, *St. Paul's Epistles to the Colossians and Philemon* (London: MacMillan, 1875), accessible in public domain on the internet at http://www.gutenberg.org/files/50857/50857-h/50857-h.htm.

As will be seen in this section, there are three specific orders of celestial beings: angels, seraphim, and cherubim.

a. Angels

The order that has been discussed in this chapter is the first, basic rank of celestial beings: the order of angels. The term "angel" is sometimes used for all orders of celestial beings, as all celestial beings are angelic beings. Most frequently, however, the term applies to the lowest of the three orders. In appearance, these beings look like young men, but they do not have wings, as they are so often portrayed.

There are two angels known by name throughout the Scriptures: Michael and Gabriel. Michael is an archangel. His name means "who is like God," and "archangel" means "chief angel." The English term comes from the Greek word *archangelos* found in I Thessalonians 4:16 and Jude 9. The concept of archangels is reflected in two other names used for Michael. In Daniel 10:13, he is called *one of the chief princes*, or in Hebrew *'aḥaḏ haśśārîm hārišōnîm*. There are many princes, but he is the first one, the one in authority over all the others. This fact is seen in Daniel 12:1, which states that Michael is called *the great prince* (Heb. *haśśār haggāḏōl*). There is only one great prince, and that is the archangel. "Great prince" and "chief prince" are his two titles in Hebrew, and they basically mean the same thing.

Michael's position means that he has specific responsibilities. As archangel, he is in authority over all other angels. He is not in authority over the seraphim and cherubim, but he rules over the lowest order, the angels. This is seen in Revelation 12:7: *And there was war in heaven: Michael and his angels going forth to war with the dragon; and the dragon warred and his angels.* Just as demons are under the authority of Satan, good angels of this category are under the authority of Michael. He is responsible for exercising rule and authority over the other angels, while the responsibility of the good angels is to submit to him. As chief prince, Michael is also responsible for the nation of Israel. According to Jude 9, it was Michael who protected the body of Moses: *But Michael the archangel, when contending with the devil he disputed about the body of Moses, did not bring against him a railing judgment, but said, The Lord rebuke you.*

In Daniel 10:13-21, Michael made certain that Daniel received the necessary revelation concerning Israel's future. According to Daniel 12:1, Michael will protect Israel during the tribulation, and indeed, the reason Israel will survive this terrible time is because of Michael's work. Other things Michael will do in the future include announcing the rapture (I Thess. 4:16), and in the middle of the tribulation, casting out Satan from his present third abode, in the atmospheric heavens, to his fourth abode, on the earth.[5] This is found in Revelation 12:7-12.

The second angel named in the Scriptures is Gabriel. In Hebrew, his name means "the mighty one of God." Gabriel's main work is to be a messenger of revelation, bringing revelation from God to man. In Daniel 8:15-27, he revealed things concerning Israel in the end days. In Daniel 9:20-27, he revealed the seventy sevens and the timing of the first coming of the Messiah. In Luke 1:11-20, he revealed the coming birth of John the Baptist to Zacharias. And in Luke 1:26-38, he revealed the coming birth of Yeshua to Miriam (Mary). Like Michael, Gabriel will also have work to do in the future. Luke 1:19 states that Gabriel is one of the angels who will *stand in the presence of God.* According to Revelation 8:2, there are seven such angels. This means that Gabriel is one of the seven who stand in the very presence of God and pour out the trumpet judgments of Revelation 8 and 9.

The Bible also mentions other individual angels. However, it omits their names. For example, as mentioned in the paragraph above, there are seven angels standing before the presence of God in Revelation 8:2, one of whom is Gabriel, but the names of the other six are not known. Revelation 15 and 16 mention seven angels who will have seven bowl judgments. Then there are the four angels of the four winds in Revelation 7:1-4, the angel of fire in Revelation 14:18, and the angel of the waters in Revelation 16:5.

b. Seraphim

The second order of celestial beings is the seraphim. The term is the plural of the Hebrew word *śārāp* (*saraph*), which means "a burning one." Seraphim are mentioned in only two books: Isaiah and Revelation. Elsewhere

---

[5] See Chapter IV: The Six Abodes of Satan.

in the Hebrew Scriptures, the term is also translated as "serpent" or "snake" (Num. 21:8; Is. 14:29; and 30:6).

In Isaiah 6:2-3 and 6-7, several things can be learned about the seraphim:

> *²Above him stood the seraphim: each one had six wings; with twain he covered his face, and with twain he covered his feet, and with twain he did fly. ³And one cried unto another, and said, Holy, holy, holy, is Jehovah of hosts: the whole earth is full of his glory . . . ⁶Then flew one of the seraphim unto me, having a live coal in his hand, which he had taken with the tongs from off the altar: ⁷and he touched my mouth with it, and said, Lo, this has touched your lips; and your iniquity is taken away, and your sin forgiven.*

According to these verses, the seraphim surround the throne of God. Unlike angels, who have no wings, seraphim are described as having six wings. Each pair has a different purpose. The purpose of the first pair is for covering their feet; the purpose of the second pair is to cover their faces; the purpose of the third pair is for flying. The verses also reveal that the seraphim praise God to each other continuously, saying over and over again: *Holy, holy, holy, is Jehovah of hosts: the whole earth is full of his glory.* One seraph is described as purifying the sins of Isaiah by taking a hot coal from the altar of sacrifice in heaven and placing it upon Isaiah's lips. At that moment, the prophet's sins were cleansed.

The rest of what can be learned about seraphim is found in the book of Revelation, where they are mentioned in eight different passages.

The first passage is Revelation 4:6-11, which states:

> *⁶and before the throne, as it were a sea of glass like unto crystal; and in the midst of the throne, and round about the throne, four living creatures full of eyes before and behind. ⁷And the first creature was like a lion, and the second creature like a calf, and the third creature had a face as of a man, and the fourth creature was like a flying eagle. ⁸And the four living creatures, having each one of them six wings, are full of eyes round about and within: and they have no rest day and night, saying, Holy, holy, holy, is the Lord God, the Almighty, who was and who is and who is to come. ⁹And when the living creatures shall give glory and honor and thanks to him that sits on*

the throne, to him that lives for ever and ever, ¹⁰the four and twenty elders shall fall down before him that sits on the throne, and shall worship him that lives for ever and ever, and shall cast their crowns before the throne, saying, ¹¹Worthy are you, our Lord and our God, to receive the glory and the honor and the power: for you did create all things, and because of your will they were, and were created.

This passage reveals seven truths about seraphim:

1. They surround the throne of God (v. 6).
2. They are full of eyes in front and back, symbolizing that they are able to see far beyond the human realm in order to be able to carry out God's providence (v. 6).
3. They have six wings (v. 8).
4. They do not all look exactly the same (v. 7). While all have six wings, the distinguishing characteristic of seraphim is differing facial features. Based upon these features, there are four categories of seraphim: lion-like, calf-like, man- or human-like, and eagle-like.
5. They are full of eyes all around. Earlier it was mentioned that they are full of eyes in front and back. Now it is stated that they are full of eyes all the way around, including the sides and within (v. 8).
6. They continuously praise God and say the same words recorded in Isaiah with a slight variation (vv. 8b-9).
7. Whenever they say, "Holy, holy, holy," it is a signal to the 24 elders that they, too, must now worship the One who sits upon the throne (vv. 10-11). In this context, the One sitting upon the throne is God the Father.

The second passage is Revelation 5:6, which states:

And I saw in the midst of the throne and of the four living creatures, and in the midst of the elders, a Lamb standing, as though it had been slain, having seven horns, and seven eyes, which are the seven Spirits of God, sent forth into all the earth.

This verse teaches that the seraphim also surround the Lamb, meaning God the Son.

The third passage is Revelation 5:8-14:

8And when he had taken the book, the four living creatures and the four and twenty elders fell down before the Lamb, having each one a harp, and golden bowls full of incense, which are the prayers of the saints. 9And they sing a new song, saying, Worthy are you to take the book, and to open the seals thereof: for you were slain, and did purchase unto God with your blood men of every tribe, and tongue, and people, and nation, 10and made them to be unto our God a kingdom and priests; and they reign upon the earth . . . 14And the four living creatures said, Amen. And the elders fell down and worshipped.

At some point in the future, the Lamb will take the seven-sealed scroll and break its seals. This act will begin the tribulation. As the Lamb takes the scroll, the seraphim will worship Him.

The fourth passage is Revelation 6:1-7:

1And And I saw when the Lamb opened one of the seven seals, and I heard one of the four living creatures saying as with a voice of thunder, Come. 2And I saw, and behold, a white horse, and he that sat thereon had a bow; and there was given unto him a crown: and he came forth conquering, and to conquer. 3And when he opened the second seal, I heard the second living creature saying, Come. 4And another horse came forth, a red horse: and to him that sat thereon it was given to take peace from the earth, and that they should slay one another: and there was given unto him a great sword. 5And when he opened the third seal, I heard the third living creature saying, Come. And I saw, and behold, a black horse; and he that sat thereon had a balance in his hand. 6And I heard as it were a voice in the midst of the four living creatures saying, A measure of wheat for a shilling, and three measures of barley for a shilling; and the oil and the wine hurt you not. 7And when he opened the fourth seal, I heard the voice of the fourth living creature saying, Come.

In these verses, the seraphim announce specific seal judgments. The first seraph announces the first seal judgment; the second seraph announces the second seal judgment; and so forth. Of the seven seal judgments, the first four will each be announced by a seraph.

The fifth passage is Revelation 7:11-12:

11And all the angels were standing round about the throne, and about the elders and the four living creatures; and they fell before the throne on their faces, and worshipped God, 12saying, Amen: Blessing, and glory, and wisdom, and thanksgiving, and honor, and power, and might, be unto our God for ever and ever. Amen.

Seraphim will be praising God for those who are saved during the tribulation, meaning the 144,000 Jews and the myriads of Gentiles.

The sixth passage is Revelation 14:3:

3and they sing as it were a new song before the throne, and before the four living creatures and the elders: and no man could learn the song save the hundred and forty and four thousand, even they that had been purchased out of the earth.

The seraphim will be witnessing 144,000 Jewish believers singing a new song in the Messianic kingdom.

The seventh passage is Revelation 15:7:

7And one of the four living creatures gave unto the seven angels seven golden bowls full of the wrath of God, who lives for ever and ever.

The judgments of Revelation 15 and 16 are by far the most severe of the tribulation judgments, and it will be a seraph who will hand these seven bowl judgments to the seven angels so that they can be poured out upon the earth.

The eighth passage is Revelation 19:4-5:

4And the four and twenty elders and the four living creatures fell down and worshipped God that sits on the throne, saying, Amen; Hallelujah. 5And a voice came forth from the throne, saying, Give praise to our God, all ye his servants, ye that fear him, the small and the great.

In these verses, seraphim lead in the worship of God.

From the Isaiah and Revelation passages, eight major truths can be deduced concerning the second order of angels:

1. The seraphim are characterized by unceasing worship of God. They worship both God the Father and God the Son.

2. They are characterized by humility. This is pictured by the fact that two wings are used to cover their feet and two wings are used to cover their faces, for they are standing in the very presence of God and surrounding His throne.

3. They have a ministry of purification of God's servants, so that these servants can also worship and serve the Lord. This is pictured in Isaiah 6:6-7 when the seraph purified the lips of the prophet.

4. The seraphim lead worship in heaven. When they say "Holy, holy, holy," all the other inhabitants of heaven, such as the 24 elders, also begin to worship God.

5. Their primary concern is to emphasize the holiness and worship of God.

6. They proclaim the holiness of God by repeating the word "holy" three times. That may very well be because of the Triunity, as the Father, the Son, and the Holy Spirit are all holy.

7. They proclaim that men need to be cleansed. This cleansing comes by means of the altar, where the shedding of blood took place. Cleansing is always by means of blood, and today (in this era of grace) it is by means of the blood of the Messiah.

8. Seraphim will be used for many of the tribulation judgments. God will use seraphim to pour out His wrath on the earth.

c. Cherubim

The third and highest order of celestial beings is the cherubim. The Hebrew word translated into English as "cherub" (singular of "cherubim") is *kərūv* (*kerub*). It comes from a word that has the root meaning of "to guard" or "to cover." The term is used a total of 91 times in the Scriptures, 27 times in the singular and 64 times in the plural. While it occurs ninety times in the Old Testament, it is found only once in the New Testament, in Hebrews 9:5.

The verses and paragraphs from the Hebrew Scriptures reveal the following truths about the cherubim:

✧ According to Genesis 3:24, cherubim guarded the entrance into the garden of Eden so that Adam and Eve could not get back in.

✧ According to Exodus 25:18-22 and 37:7-9, cherubim covered the mercy seat.

✧ According to Exodus 26:1, figures of cherubim were embroidered into the curtains of the Tabernacle.

✧ In I Samuel 4:4, II Samuel 6:2, II Kings 19:15, I Chronicles 13:6, Psalm 80:1, 99:1, and Isaiah 37:16, God is pictured as sitting above the cherubim.

✧ According to II Samuel 22:11 and Psalm 18:10, Yeshua the Messiah will be riding a cherub at His second coming.

✧ According to I Kings 6:23-28, 7:29, and 7:36, cherubim are made for the holy of holies of the Solomonic Temple. These cherubim each have two wings.

✧ According to I Kings 8:6-7, I Chronicles 28:18, and II Chronicles 5:7-8, cherubim covered the ark of the covenant in the Temple.

✧ According to II Chronicles 3:7, they were engraved on the walls of the Temple.

✧ According to II Chronicles 3:10-14, there were images of cherubim in the holy of holies. They each had two wings. They were also embroidered into the veil that separated the holy of holies from the holy place.

The Prophet Ezekiel provided the most details concerning cherubim and explained just how God sits above them. In Ezekiel 1:5-28, the prophet made eleven points:

1. The basic *likeness* of cherubim is that *of a man* (v. 5).

2. Each cherub has four different faces (v. 6) that are detailed in verse 10 as the faces of a man, a lion, an ox, and an eagle. In this area, they resemble the seraphim.

3. Each cherub has four wings, two on each side of the body (v. 6).

4. Their feet are absolutely *straight* (v. 7).

5. The soles of their feet are *like the sole of a calf's foot* (v. 7).

6. They sparkle *like burnished brass* (v. 7).

7. They have *the hands of a man under their wings on their four sides* (v. 8).

8. They appear in four ways: *like burnished brass*; *like burning coals of fire*; like *torches*; and *fire* is in their midst (v. 13).

9. They travel with the speed of *a flash of lightning* (v. 14).

10. The *noise of their wings* is like *great waters, like the voice of the Almighty, a noise of tumult like the noise of a host* (v. 24).

11. They are connected or closely associated with the Shechinah glory (vv. 26-28).

According to Ezekiel 10:1-22, the cherubim were involved in the departure of the Shechinah glory.

Ezekiel 28:14-16 states that Satan was a cherub when he was created. In fact, he was the anointed cherub. Just as Michael is the archangel, the one in authority over all the other angels, Satan was the "archcherub," the one in authority over all the other cherubim. Since the cherubim are the highest order, this made him of a higher category than Michael.

The last place cherubim are mentioned in the Hebrew Scriptures is Ezekiel 41, in verses 18-20 and 25. According to these verses, in the future, the figures of the cherubim will be engraved on the walls of the Millennial Temple. These cherubim will have two faces: one of a man and one of a young lion. Their figures will also be engraved on the doors of the Millennial Temple.

In the New Testament, Hebrews 9:5 reiterates the teaching of the Hebrew Scriptures by stating: *and above it cherubim of glory overshadowing the mercy-seat; of which things we cannot now speak severally.* The mercy seat the cherubim overshadowed was that of the Tabernacle.

From these passages, seven major truths can be deduced about the cherubim.

1. There are three different types or categories of cherubim: those who have only one face and two wings; those who have two faces and two wings; and those who have four faces and four wings. It is never stated exactly which kind of cherub Satan is, but we know that he is in one of these three categories.

2. These beings are closely related to the throne of God in that they are the ones who carry the throne (Ez. 1). Whereas the seraphim surround the throne, the cherubim actually carry the throne and also cover it from above. For this reason, it is stated that God is the One who sits above the cherubim. The cherubim, then, are closely related to the throne of God; this closer proximity to the throne itself is the reason they are of a higher order than the seraphim.

3. They are very closely related to the Shechinah glory. To a great extent, they reflect the Shechinah glory. They were involved in the departure of the Shechinah glory from Israel in 586 B.C. before the Temple was destroyed by the Babylonians.

4. The cherubim are closely related to the visible manifestation of God's presence. This point is tied into their connection to the Shechinah glory.

5. While the seraphim are concerned with the worship and holiness of God, the cherubim are concerned with the justice, power, and might of God.

6. The cherubim defend God's holy character and presence. This is the reason they need their might.

7. They have the ability to carry out God's will swiftly among the nations.

d. Summarizing the Hierarchy In the Angelic Realm

The following chart provides a visual aid to understand the order of celestial beings.

(Satan the archcherub)
Cherubim

Seraphim

Michael the archangel
Angels

J. The Works of Angels

The works of angels will be discussed in seven different categories: in relation to God, as agents of revelation, in the life of the Messiah, among the nations, among unbelievers, in relation to believers, and in the future.

1. The Work of Angels in Relation to God

One of the ministries of angels in relation to God is that they are employed in His worship. They are seen as actively worshipping God in Psalm 29:1-2; 103:20; 148:2; Isaiah 6:3; Hebrews 1:6; Revelation 4:8-11; and 5:8-13. Of interest is that the Revelation 4 passage speaks of their worship of God the Father, while the Revelation 5 passage speaks of their worship of God the Son.

Angels also execute God's will. This point is brought out in Psalm 103:20 and Hebrews 1:7.

The Scriptures present angels as rejoicing in the work of God. When God created the heavens and earth, the angels shouted for joy (Job 38:7). When God saves an individual, there is joy among the angels (Lk. 15:10).

Finally, angels are seen executing God's judgments. In Genesis 19:1-22, they were used to destroy Sodom and Gomorrah. In Exodus 12:23, they were used in connection with the tenth plague in Egypt. In I Chronicles 21:15, they were used in connection with the pestilence in Israel.

2. The Work of Angels as Agents of Revelation

Moses did receive some of the law directly, but much of it was mediated to him by means of angels. This is hinted at in Deuteronomy 33:2, and it was part of rabbinic tradition. Not all rabbinic traditions are verified by the New Testament, but this case is, as can be seen in Acts 7:53, Galatians 3:19, and Hebrews 2:2. Furthermore, while Daniel often received his revelation directly from God, some of his material (such as Daniel 8:1-12:13) came by means of angels. The same thing is true of Zechariah. Zechariah's book has 14 chapters, but the first six of these chapters, Zechariah 1:7-6:15, came by means of angels. The book of Revelation, written by the

Apostle John, was mediated and revealed to him by means of an angel according to Revelation 1:1; 10:1-11; 17:1; 19:9-10; 21:9; and 22:16.

3. The Work of Angels in the Life of the Messiah

Angels were used in five specific instances in the life of the Messiah. The first occasion was the time of His birth and early life. It was an angel who predicted the birth of the Messiah to Miriam (Mary) in Luke 1:26-38 and to Joseph in Matthew 1:20-23. Angels were used in Luke 2:8-15 to announce the birth of the Messiah to the Jewish shepherds outside Bethlehem. It was an angel who warned Joseph in Matthew 2:13 to flee Bethlehem; and an angel told Joseph in Matthew 2:19-20 to leave Egypt and return to Israel.

The second period was during the ministry of Yeshua, something that was predicted in Psalm 91:1-12 and affirmed by Paul in I Timothy 3:16. When Yeshua was tempted, angels were used to minister to Him (Mt. 4:11; Mk. 1:13). They were *ascending and descending upon the Son of man* throughout His ministry (Jn. 1:51). They ministered to Yeshua during His agony in the garden of Gethsemane (Lk. 22:43). Finally, according to Matthew 26:53, there were *more than twelve legions of angels* ready to defend Yeshua at His trial if He needed them for any purpose, which, of course, He did not.

The third occasion when angels were used in the life of the Messiah was in connection with the resurrection. It was an angel who *rolled away the stone* from the tomb (Mt. 28:2). Angels were used to announce the resurrection to the women who came to the tomb (Mt. 28:1-7; Mk. 16:5-7; Lk. 24:4-7; Jn. 20:12-13).

The fourth instance was at the ascension. After Messiah ascended into heaven, angels announced in Acts 1:10-11 that this same Yeshua, who was then departing, would come again *in like manner*. The phrase means that He will return someday just as He left, namely, in the clouds of heaven.

The fifth setting is still future. Angels will come with the Messiah in the clouds of heaven at His second coming. This is found in Matthew 16:27; 24:31; 25:31; and II Thessalonians 1:7. Therefore, even in the future, angels will be involved in the life of the Messiah.

4. The Work of Angels Among the Nations

Two things should be mentioned concerning the work of angels among the nations. First, angelic beings function in the capacity of "cosmocrats," meaning they function as world rulers or as rulers of nations. Daniel 10:13, for example, mentions a leading angelic being, *the prince of the kingdom of Persia*. According to Daniel 10:21 and 12:1, the archangel Michael not only has authority over the other angels, but also happens to be the chief prince over Israel.

Second, angels are also closely associated with the humans who rule over specific nations. Isaiah 14:3-20 is a good example of this fact. In this passage, Isaiah mentioned the human king of Babylon (vv. 3-11). Then, he turned his attention to Satan (vv. 12-14), followed by a renewed mention of the king of Babylon (vv. 15-20). The same thing is true of Ezekiel 28:1-19, which speaks about Tyre. Verses 1-10 speak of the human prince of Tyre, while verses 11-19 are addressed to Satan as the king of Tyre.

Because both fallen and unfallen angelic beings are used as cosmocrats or world rulers, they carry out God's will among the nations. Many things that happen among nations are due to these angelic beings. Quite frequently, the reason nations go to war against one another is because they have been moved to do so by these cosmocratic angelic beings.

5. The Work of Angels Among Unbelievers

Concerning the work of angels among unbelievers, three facets should be noted. First, angels announce impending judgment. Historically, this was done in Genesis 19:12-13, when angels announced the coming destruction of Sodom and Gomorrah. In the future, they will do so again as they announce the terrible bowl judgments in Revelation 14:6-7.

Second, angels are used to inflict punishment. This fact may be seen in the Exodus account, where an angel carried out the tenth plague upon the firstborn sons of the Egyptians (Ex. 12:23). Other examples are found in II Samuel 24:16 and Ezekiel 9:1-8. A New Testament example is Acts 12:23, when an angel was used to smite Herod Agrippa with a fatal disease. What angels have done in the past, they will also do in the future during the tribulation (Rev. 8:1-2, 6; 16:1).

Third, at the end of the tribulation, angels will act as "reapers," separating believers from unbelievers (Mt. 13:39-42, 49-50).

6. The Work of Angels in Relation to Believers

From the many passages of Scripture that speak of the work of angels in relation to believers, nine things should be mentioned. First, these elect, holy angels rejoice when someone is saved (Lk. 15:10), while fallen angels do not rejoice.

Second, angels exercise guardianship over believers, meaning they carry out general protective care. Psalms 34:7 and 91:11 teach that nothing can happen to a believer because of the general protective care of angels. Matthew 18:10 teaches that all children have guardian angels, and Hebrews 1:14 states that every believer has a guardian angel as well. In fact, as soon as one is saved, a guardian angel is assigned to him. When bad things do happen to a believer, it is not because the angels were failing at their jobs, but because it was God's permissive will.

Third, angels are often used to save or rescue believers from specific situations. For example, angels were used in Genesis 19:1-22 to rescue Lot. In Genesis 32:1-2, angels were used to aid Jacob. In I Kings 19:5-6, an angel was used to feed the Prophet Elijah. In II Kings 6:17, angels protected Elijah. In Daniel 3:24-28, an angel protected Shadrach, Meshach, and Abednego in the fiery furnace. In Daniel 6:22, an angel shut the mouths of the lions so that no harm came to Daniel. In Acts 5:17-20, an angel rescued the apostles. Finally, an angel rescued Peter in Acts 12:6-11.

Fourth, angels also guide believers into truth and actions. For example, in Matthew 1:20-23, an angel instructed Joseph to believe Miriam's story that she really was a virgin, even though she was already pregnant. In Acts 8:26, an angel brought Philip to the Ethiopian eunuch. In Acts 10:3-8, an angel instructed Cornelius to send for Peter so that he might preach the gospel to him. The same point is reaffirmed in Acts 11:13-14. In Acts 27:23-24, an angel guided Paul as well.

Fifth, sometimes prayers are answered by means of angels. In the case of Daniel, for example, this happened twice. An angel was used in Daniel 9:20-23 and again in 10:12-13 to answer the prophet's prayer for more revelation. In the New Testament, groups of saints were praying for Peter's release from prison. In answer to their prayers, an angel was used to rescue the apostle (Acts 12:1-19).

Sixth, angels are used to encourage believers. This is seen in Acts 5:18-20 and 27:23-25.

Seventh, angels carry the soul to its abode in heaven when a believer dies. This is seen in Luke 16:22.

Eighth, angels serve as spectators of believers. They have the ministry of observation to see how believers are acting and responding. For example, in Luke 12:8, the faith of a believer is confessed before the angels. Later, in Luke 15:10, angels observe when one is saved. Angels also observe the sufferings of believers, as seen in I Corinthians 4:9. In I Corinthians 11:10, angels observe whether or not women are obedient in wearing the head covering in the church. In I Timothy 5:21, angels are present when believers make a commitment to the Lord. Finally, according to I Peter 1:10-12, angels observe and look into God's work of salvation.

Ninth, angels serve as guardians over local churches. This is seen in Revelation 2 and 3, where each letter is addressed to the angel of this church or that church.

In light of the angels' ministry to believers, believers may respond in the following manners. They are allowed to wonder and be amazed at the angels' ability and work, like Daniel in Daniel 8:16-17 and 10:1-9. Believers can appreciate the angels' ministry, as seen in Hebrews 1:14. However, they are forbidden to worship angels (Col. 2:18; Rev. 19:10; 22:9). In the future, believers will judge fallen angels at the Great White Throne Judgment (I Cor. 6:3).

7. The Work of Angels in the Future

During the tribulation, the angels will perform seven specific works:

1. After the 144,000 Jews have been sealed, angels will be used to cause damage upon the earth as part of God's divine judgment (Rev. 7:1-3). The sealing will protect these Jewish witnesses from any harm.

2. Seven angels will be used to pour out the seven trumpet judgments (Rev. 8:1-9:21; 11:15-19).

3. In the middle of the tribulation, good angels will be used to cast Satan and the fallen angels out of their present abode in the atmospheric heavens to be confined to the earth for the rest of the tribulation (Rev. 12:7-12).

4. Angels will make certain midtribulational announcements (Rev. 14:6-20).

5. Just as angels are going to be used to pour out the trumpet judgments, they will be used to pour out the bowl judgments (Rev. 15:7-16:21).

6. Also during the tribulation, an angel will be used to pass the sentence of destruction upon the city of Babylon (Rev. 18:1-3, 21-24).

7. Angels will be used in the context of the Campaign of Armageddon (Rev. 19:17-18).

The unfallen angels are also seen in connection with Messiah's second coming. They will return with Him at the second coming, as can be seen in Matthew 16:27; 24:31; 25:31; and II Thessalonians 1:7. Furthermore, as previously mentioned, they will separate believers from unbelievers at the second coming. This is confirmed in Matthew 13:39-42, 49-50.

The unfallen angels will also play an important role during the Messianic kingdom. One of them, a common angel, will receive the authority to bind Satan in the abyss for 1,000 years (Rev. 20:1-3). The mighty anointed cherub will be humbled by the fact that he will be bound by an unnamed angel of the lowest order. Angels will also be used to regather the Jews back into the land of Israel (Mt. 24:31).

Finally, the future work of angels includes a role in the eternal state and the eternal order. According to Revelation 21:12, angels will serve as guardians of the city gates. The New Jerusalem, which will be the eternal abode of all believers of all time, will have twelve gates, three on each side of the city. Each gate will be made of a huge pearl and each will be guarded by an angel.

K. The Destiny of Angels

Hebrews 12:22 states: *but ye are come unto mount Zion, and unto the city of the living God, the heavenly Jerusalem, and to innumerable hosts of angels.* According to this verse, the destiny of all good angels is the same as that of all the saints of all time: the New Jerusalem. All the elect, holy angels, those who did not fall with Satan, will have their eternal abode in the New Jerusalem.

L. Questions and Study Suggestions

Study Suggestion 1: A common definition of angels is: "Angels are created, spiritual beings with moral judgment and high intelligence, but without physical bodies."

> ➤ List two verses that prove that angels are created beings.
> ➤ List the attributes that prove that angels have personality.
> ➤ List two verses that prove they are spiritual beings.
> ➤ How would you prove from the Scriptures that these beings are capable of moral judgment?
> ➤ Which verse proves that they do not have physical bodies?

Question 1: What is the meaning of the Hebrew and the Greek words for "angel"? Which verse shows that the term is also used for humans?

Question 2: Regarding angels being guardians of people, how do you prove this from the Scriptures? Reflect on what this truth means to you personally.

Question 3: What is the difference between angels, seraphim, and cherubim? When you describe the differences, make sure to include details about their ranks and their appearances.

Question 4: In the Scriptures, the word "star" is used symbolically for angels. Find the exception to the rule and explain who or what is meant by the symbol in the verse.

Fill in the blanks: We discussed five options to explain the fact that Yeshua taught the existence of angels. Fill in the blanks:

a. Yeshua Himself was _____; He didn't _____ any better.

b. Yeshua was _____; although He knew better, He went ahead and taught _____.

c. Yeshua taught about angels to _____ the belief held by _____.

d. The Gospel writers themselves _____, which He never really said.

e. The only logical, correct option: _____.

Word Search: Find all names for angels in the below word search.

F	R	R	T	S	O	T	A	S	Y	B	A	R	N	S
O	E	O	A	L	N	R	R	H	T	H	E	A	E	J
G	N	S	W	T	W	A	T	C	H	E	R	R	S	R
T	O	R	U	T	S	T	E	E	G	D	A	I	P	E
T	O	E	S	E	R	O	M	T	I	W	W	E	S	E
H	E	T	G	E	L	O	H	I	M	E	A	E	H	O
V	O	S	H	O	L	Y	O	N	E	S	T	T	S	V
S	T	I	R	I	P	S	A	R	H	S	C	L	O	E
N	O	N	O	N	L	N	E	H	T	F	H	D	N	E
F	R	I	E	E	E	H	T	O	F	E	M	O	N	A
E	S	M	N	U	G	N	I	O	O	O	A	N	H	P
Y	E	I	S	T	N	R	E	G	S	R	N	T	E	T
V	A	L	B	I	A	C	N	G	N	I	R	R	N	L
T	E	E	Y	H	D	O	G	F	O	S	N	O	S	K
G	H	O	C	N	A	F	E	S	S	T	E	S	U	E

Part 2:

Satanology

Chapter II

The Angel of Darkness

The purpose of the study of Satanology is to dispel many of the false views that are held concerning Satan, the "angel of darkness." One such misconception is that Satan is not a personality, but only an evil principle with which all must wrestle. Another false view is that he is the direct cause of every sin in every individual, so that when someone with this view sins, he always blames it on the devil. Also erroneous is to believe that Satan or one of his demons is responsible for every physical and mental disorder.

This chapter will deal with the doctrine of Satan by looking at the existence of Satan, his origin, his personality, the designations of Satan, and his nature.

A. The Existence of Satan

Satan is mentioned in seven of the 39 books of the Hebrew Scriptures, namely in Genesis, I Chronicles, Job, Psalms, Isaiah, Ezekiel, and Zechariah. He is also mentioned in 19 of the 27 books of the New Testament: Matthew, Mark, Luke, John, Acts, Romans, I and II Corinthians, Ephesians, I and II Thessalonians, I and II Timothy, Hebrews, James, I Peter, I John, Jude, and Revelation. While Satan is not mentioned in every New Testament book, he is mentioned by every New Testament writer. While the sheer number of verses that speak of or deal with Satan is proof of his existence, the most important evidence comes from the Messiah Himself. In the four Gospels, He mentioned Satan 25 times. There are only four additional verses in the Gospels that speak of the devil without being a direct quote of Messiah's words.

The following verses are examples from each Gospel where Yeshua taught the existence of Satan:

✿   Matthew 4:10: *Then says Yeshua unto him, Get you hence, Satan: for it is written, You shall worship the Lord your God, and him only shall you serve.*

✿   Mark 3:26: *And if Satan has risen up against himself, and is divided, he cannot stand, but has an end.*

✿   Luke 13:16: *And ought not this woman, being a daughter of Abraham, whom Satan had bound, lo, these eighteen years, to have been loosed from this bond on the day of the sabbath?*

✿   John 12:31: *Now is the judgment of this world: now shall the prince of this world be cast out.*

There is no question that the Bible teaches the existence of Satan both in the Hebrew Scriptures and the New Testament. He is not merely an imaginary character or emanation, and he is more than just an evil principle. He is a real being. Not only is Satan mentioned in the apocalyptic or visionary books that deal with many symbols (such as Revelation), he is also mentioned in the prophetic and the historical books as well.

B. The Origin of Satan: Ezekiel 28:11-15

Ezekiel 28:11-15 provides the key information regarding the origin of the angel of darkness. This passage will be discussed in detail in Chapter III of this book. For now, a summary will concentrate on the fact that Satan is a created being.

According to verses 11-12, Satan is deemed the wisest and the most beautiful of celestial beings. When he was created, he sealed up the sum in the two areas of wisdom and beauty. More will be said about this in Chapter III.

Verse 13 makes the point that Satan is a created being. He did not exist for all eternity past. Hence, he is not "the eternal evil principle" that always existed alongside "the eternal good principle." He is a real being who was created by God. At the time of his creation, two things were true of him. First, he had a covering of stones, which made him the "shining one." Second, he was in charge of the tabrets (tambourines) and pipes, which are instruments involved in worship. Satan is pictured as the priest in heaven, leading the worship of God.[6]

According to verse 14, Satan was created a cherub. Furthermore, he was *the anointed cherub*. When he was first created, he was a cherub co-equal with all other cherubs. But at some point, God selected this particular cherub and anointed or "messiahed" him. This made Satan the "archcherub" and put him in authority over the other cherubs.

According to verse 15, Satan was created without a single flaw. He was perfect. Furthermore, he possessed a unique ability called "the power of contrary choice." This power is the ability to choose contrary to one's nature. God does not have that ability, which is why God cannot sin; He cannot go contrary to His divine nature. Satan was holy and perfect, but he had the ability to make an imperfect and unholy choice.

What Ezekiel teaches about the origin of Satan can be summarized in five points:

1. Satan is a created being; therefore, he did not exist eternally.

2. He was created perfect, without a single flaw.

3. He was created a cherub, the highest order of celestial beings.

4. By sealing up the sum in wisdom and beauty, he was the wisest and the most beautiful of all created beings.

5. Being the anointed cherub meant that he was the highest in power and authority of all created beings.

C. The Personality of Satan

1. The Attributes of Personality

There are many false teachings that picture Satan as an emanation or an evil principle, not as a real person. Yet, the fact that the angel of darkness

---

[6] More will be said about this interpretation of Ezekiel 28:13 in Chapter IV.

has all three attributes of personality—intellect, emotion, and will—proves the opposite is true.

Satan's intellect is seen in several passages of Scripture. In Job 1 and 2, he debates with God over the righteousness of Job, and that shows intellect. In Matthew 4:6, he is able to quote Scripture. In Luke 4:1-12, he is able to carry on a conversation with Yeshua. In II Corinthians 11:3, he is described as being crafty, a function of the intellect. In Ephesians 6:11, Paul writes about the schemes or ruses of the devil. All this shows clearly that Satan has intellect, the first attribute of personality.

Satan also has emotion. According to I Timothy 3:6, he has the ability to be puffed up; that is, he has the capacity to be filled with the emotion of pride. Furthermore, verses 12 and 17 of Revelation 12 speak of the wrath of Satan, which is the emotion of anger. So, Satan has emotion as well as intellect.

Finally, Satan is described as having will. In Isaiah 14:13-14, Satan declared five times, "I will." Luke 4:6-7 states that Satan has the power to give the kingdoms of the world to whomsoever he wills. II Timothy 2:26 speaks of people being taken captive to do Satan's will. In I Peter 5:8, Satan is portrayed as one who is looking for and choosing his victims, and his choice is made on the basis of his will.

That which characterizes personality are the three attributes of intellect, emotion, and will, and Satan has all three attributes.

2. The Use of Personal Pronouns

In the Hebrew language, there is no such thing as a neuter gender; every word is either in the masculine or the feminine form. Even things we consider neuter in English, such as tables and chairs, are given either a masculine or a feminine gender in Hebrew. Thus, the Hebrew is inconclusive on Satan. However, the Greek language has all three genders: masculine, feminine, and neuter. If Satan were merely a thing and not a personality, neuter pronouns would have been used consistently in reference to him. But everywhere Satan is mentioned in the Greek New Testament, he is always referred to as "he," "him," or "his," but never as "it."

The use of the Greek masculine pronoun shows the gender of Satan, and this confirms that he is a personality.

3. The Actions of a Personality

Satan performs all of the actions of a personality and therefore does not act like a thing. As mentioned, the Apostle John wrote in I John 3:8: *he that does sin is of the devil; for the devil sins from the beginning.* The fact that Satan has been sinning from the beginning shows the action of a personality, because things do not sin.

In I Chronicles 21:1, Satan is portrayed as being able to stand against something and to move people to do his bidding: *And Satan stood up against Israel, and moved David to number Israel.*

In Zechariah 3:1, he is pictured as an adversary, a prosecuting attorney: *And he showed me Joshua the high priest standing before the angel of Jehovah, and Satan standing at his right hand to be his adversary.*

According to John 8:44, Satan is able to lust, lie, and murder: *Ye are of your father the devil, and the lusts of your father it is your will to do. He was a murderer from the beginning, and stands not in the truth, because there is no truth in him. When he speaks a lie, he speaks of his own: for he is a liar, and the father thereof.*

In Hebrews 2:14, Satan is pictured as having power and authority: *Since then the children are sharers in flesh and blood, he also himself in like manner partook of the same; that through death he might bring to nought him that had the power of death, that is, the devil.*

All of these verses clearly show that Satan performs the actions of a personality.

4. His Treatment as a Morally Responsible Individual

The Scriptures treat Satan as a morally responsible individual. One example of this truth is Matthew 25:41, which states: *Then shall he say also unto them on the left hand, Depart from me, ye cursed, into the eternal fire which is prepared for the devil and his angels.* Satan is destined for the lake of fire. Neuter things are not cast into the lake of fire, but personalities are. The fact that Satan is destined for the lake of fire shows that the Scriptures treat him as a morally responsible being.

John 16:11 makes a similar point: *the prince of this world has been judged*. This, too, shows that Satan is treated as a morally responsible being. This means that he is a personality.

D. The Designations of Satan

There are many designations of Satan found throughout the Scriptures. They can be categorized into four groups: names, titles, descriptions, and representations.

1. Names

Altogether, the Bible gives four names of the angel of darkness. The most common name is *Satan*, which in Hebrew is *śāṭān* (*satan*). It is used 19 times in the Hebrew Scriptures. One instance of this usage is Job 2:1: *Again it came to pass on the day when the sons of God came to present themselves before Jehovah, that Satan came also among them to present himself before Jehovah*. The Greek form of the name is *Satanas*. It is used 36 times in the Greek New Testament. One instance of this usage is Revelation 12:9: *And the great dragon was cast down, the old serpent, he that is called the Devil and Satan, the deceiver of the whole world; he was cast down to the earth, and his angels were cast down with him*. The name means "adversary" or "resistor" and emphasizes Satan as the leader of the rival kingdom of the kingdom of God.

Satan's second name is *Devil*. The Greek word is *diabolos*, which is used 35 times in the Greek New Testament. One example of this usage is the above quoted Revelation 12:9. The word means "accuser," "slanderer," "one who trips up." This name pictures Satan as one who defames both God and the believer.

Satan's third name is *Belial*. It is found in II Corinthians 6:15: *And what concord has Messiah with Belial? or what portion has a believer with an unbeliever?* The name Belial means "worthlessness." This gives God's view of the fallen creature, Satan.

Satan's fourth name is *Beelzebub*. The original form of the name was *Beelzebul*, meaning, "the lord of the royal palace." According to II Kings 1:2, 3, 6, and 16, he was the god of the Philistine city of Ekron. After the

Jews had finally been cured of idolatry by the Babylonian Captivity, the rabbis liked to poke fun at various pagan gods and apply some of their names to different demons. Here, they changed the last letter so that the name became Beelzebub, meaning "the lord of the flies" or "the lord of the dung." According to the rabbis, Beelzebub was the demon in charge of diseases. By New Testament times, it had become a name for Satan. Beelzebub is found in Matthew 10:25; 12:24, 27; Mark 3:22; Luke 11:15, 18, and 19.

2. Titles

Altogether, the Scriptures provide ten specific titles of Satan. The first title is *day-star, son of the morning*. It is found in Isaiah 14:12. The Hebrew word for "day-star" is *hêlêl* (*helel*). It means "the shining one." The Latin translation of this term is *lucifer*, and this word appears in the Vulgate. However, the correct reading in English should not be Lucifer, for that is never a biblical name for Satan, nor is it a biblical title. The correct title is "day-star, son of the morning," or in Hebrew *hêlêl bên šāḥar*. It emphasizes how Satan was in his original state. According to Ezekiel 28, he was the shining one, covered by the precious stones. He can still appear as an angel of light (II Cor. 11:14).

Satan's second title is *the destroyer*. In Hebrew, this title is *'ăḇaddōwn* (*avadon*), and in Greek, it is *Apollyon*. This title is found in Revelation 9:11: *They have over them as king the angel of the abyss: his name in Hebrew is Abaddon, and in the Greek tongue he has the name Apollyon.* The meaning of both the Hebrew and the Greek words is "destroyer" because Satan is the destroyer of both physical and spiritual life.[7]

Satan's third title is *the prince of this world*. It is found in John 12:31; 14:30; and 16:11. The Greek term for "world" is *kosmos*, which is Satan's counterpart to God's kingdom and rule. Satan is the prince of the cosmos, just as the Messiah is the Prince of God's kingdom. This title pictures Satan as carrying out his fifth "I will" statement: to be like God. It is a reference to the carrying out of his counterfeit program.

---

[7] There is a possibility that Revelation 9:11 speaks of a chief demon rather than Satan. But if it does refer to Satan, then it pictures him as a destroyer.

Satan's fourth title is *the prince of the powers of the air*. It is found in Ephesians 2:2: *wherein ye once walked according to the course of this world, according to the prince of the powers of the air, of the spirit that now works in the sons of disobedience*. According to this verse, the title emphasizes two things: It emphasizes Satan in his third abode, the atmospheric heavens; and it emphasizes his authority over the other angels that fell with him. He is the prince of the powers, or the fallen angels.

Satan's fifth title is *the god of this age*. It is found in II Corinthians 4:4: *in whom the god of this world has blinded the minds of the unbelieving, that the light of the gospel of the glory of Messiah, who is the image of God, should not dawn upon them*. Here, the Greek word for "world" is not *kosmos*, but *aión*, which means "age." It emphasizes the system of philosophy that is contrary to God and is the spirit of this age and this cosmos. In Ephesians 2:2, the Greek phrase for "the course of this world" is *aiōna tou kosmou*, which basically means "the age of this cosmos." Hence, Satan is the prince of this cosmos, and he propagates a philosophy in the cosmos that is the characteristic of this age. According to Galatians 1:4, believers have been delivered from *this present evil world [aiōnos]*, meaning they have been delivered from the system of philosophy that is the spirit of this age. So, the title "god of this age" emphasizes the satanic philosophy in the outworking of Satan's control of the cosmos.

Satan's sixth title is *the evil one*. It is found in Matthew 6:13; John 17:15; II Thessalonians 3:3; and I John 5:18-19. The Greek word for "evil one" is *ponéros*, which emphasizes Satan's corrupted nature. In his nature, he is the evil one and the source of evil.

Satan's seventh title is *the anointed cherub that covers*. It is found in Ezekiel 28:14, a verse that was previously dealt with. The title emphasizes two things. First, it reveals to which order of celestial beings Satan belongs: He is a cherub. Second, it emphasizes Satan's unique position; he was *the anointed cherub that covers*. Other cherubs are holding the throne of God. They are underneath it, and that is why God is sometimes described as the One who sits above the cherubim. But at one time, Satan was the covering cherub. He was the one that served as the canopy over the throne of God. All the other cherubs were under it, but Satan, as the anointed cherub, was over God's throne.

Satan's eighth title is *the prince of demons*. It is found in Matthew 12:24 and Luke 11:15 and emphasizes his authority over the angels who fell with him.

Satan's ninth title is *the king of Tyre*. It is found in Ezekiel 28:11-12 and pictures him in control over the earthly kingdoms of this world.

Satan's tenth title is *the king of Babylon*. It is found in Isaiah 14:4, which also emphasizes his control over nations.

3. Descriptions

There are five descriptions of Satan in the Scriptures. First, he is described as *the accuser of the brethren* (Rev. 12:10). Whenever a believer falls into a state of unconfessed sin, sooner or later Satan will appear before the throne of God, accusing this believer of that specific sin. This is why believers still need the ministry of Yeshua as their advocate. Whenever Satan has any grounds for accusing a believer, the Messiah can then say, "Lay this sin upon my account; I have already paid for it when I died for that person on the cross."

Two examples where Satan is seen as the accuser of the brethren are found in the book of Job. Job 1:9-11 states:

> *⁹Then Satan answered Jehovah, and said, Does Job fear God for nought? ¹⁰Have not you made a hedge about him, and about his house, and about all that he has, on every side? you have blessed the work of his hands, and his substance is increased in the land. ¹¹But put forth your hand now, and touch all that he has, and he will renounce you to your face.*

Satan accused Job of being righteous before God only because God had blessed him. In other words, Satan accused Job of wrong motives.

He did so again in Job 2:4-5:

> *⁴And Satan answered Jehovah, and said, Skin for skin, yea, all that a man has will he give for his life. ⁵But put forth your hand now, and touch his bone and his flesh, and he will renounce you to your face.*

Satan claimed that a person will do anything to save his life, and that included Job. Satan not only accuses individual saints before God, but also Israel as a nation. An example of this is found in Zechariah 3:1-2.

Second, Satan is described as *the angel of light*. This description is found in II Corinthians 11:14: *And no marvel; for even Satan fashions himself into an angel of light*. The description emphasizes Satan's deceptive character and is another outworking of the fifth "I will" statement: "I will make myself like the Most High." Satan has set up a counterfeit program and appears as a counterfeit angel of light. In reality, Satan is the angel of darkness, but he fashions himself to appear as an angel of light, because he wants to deceive. Being mistaken for an angel of light is the most successful way Satan deceives.

Third, Satan is described as *the tempter*. The description is found in Matthew 4:3: *And the tempter came and said unto him, If you are the Son of God, command that these stones become bread*. It is also found in I Thessalonians 3:5. The Greek word for "tempter" is *peirazōn*. The word is a present participle that pictures Satan in his present activity as going around tempting people. The description emphasizes him as one who entices men to evil and as one who tries men in moral combat. He tempts people to commit acts of sin, in particular, the sin of immorality.

Fourth, Satan is described as *the deceiver*. This description is found in Revelation 12:9: *the old serpent, he that is called the Devil and Satan, the deceiver of the whole world*. The Greek word here is *planōn*, which is a present participle that emphasizes what Satan is constantly doing: He is continually going around deceiving. This is the carrying out of his fifth "I will."

Fifth, Satan is described as *the spirit that now works in the sons of disobedience*. This description is found in Ephesians 2:2 and it emphasizes two things: First, Satan is a spirit being; second, as a spirit being, he works particularly among a certain segment of the children of men, *the sons of disobedience*, that is, among nonbelievers. At one time, all human beings were in this category, but now believers have been redeemed from the kingdom of darkness into the kingdom of the light of the Son of God. Satan no longer works in them, but he does work against them.

4. Representations

There are three animal-like representations of Satan in the Scriptures. The first representation is *the serpent*. It is found in Genesis 3:1: *Now the serpent was more subtle than any beast of the field which Jehovah God had made.* In the first reference to him in Scripture, Satan appeared as a serpent or as having "indwelled" a serpent to deceive Eve. This representation is found again in Genesis 3:2, 4, 13, 14; II Corinthians 11:3; Revelation 12:9, 15; and 20:2. It emphasizes Satan's craftiness. Just as the serpent was the most subtle of all beings God created in Genesis 3:1, even so, Satan is the craftiest of all personalities in the sinful state.

The second representation of Satan is *the great red dragon*. It is found in Revelation 12:3: *There was seen another sign in heaven: and behold, a great red dragon, having seven heads and ten horns, and upon his heads seven diadems.* The same expression is found in Revelation 12:4, 7, 9, 13, and 17. While paintings of Satan in a red suit with a tail and a pitchfork certainly do not show his real appearance, there is some truth to them. In the above quoted verse, Satan is described as being red, and as a dragon, he certainly would have a tail (but not a pitchfork). However, the Greek term for "dragon," *drakōn*, simply emphasizes Satan's power and ferocity.

The third representation of Satan is *a roaring lion*. It is found in I Peter 5:8: *Be sober, be watchful: your adversary the devil, as a roaring lion, walks about, seeking whom he may devour.* The emphasis here is on Satan's destructiveness. He is out to destroy.

E. The Nature of Satan

There are seven aspects of the nature of Satan. Some of these aspects will repeat what has already been said. However, they need to be mentioned again because in the context of the nature of Satan, they reveal new information.

The first aspect of Satan's nature is that he is a creature, not a creator who can create out of nothing. This truth is brought out in Ezekiel 28:15 and Colossians 1:16. This means Satan has not existed for all eternity, but he had an actual beginning.

Second, Satan is a *cherub*. This fact is stated in Ezekiel 28:14 and 16. By his nature as a cherub, Satan is of a higher order than the seraphim and the angels.

Third, Satan is of the first rank of angels. He was not just a cherub. According to Ezekiel 28:14, he used to be *the anointed cherub*. This anointing meant that he had authority over those of his own cherubic order. The point is that with this anointing, Satan became the archcherub, the one in authority over all the other cherubs, just as Michael was the archangel, the one in authority over all the other angels. According to Jude 8-9, even Michael had to respect Satan:

> *8Yet in like manner these also in their dreamings defile the flesh, and set at nought dominion, and rail at dignities. 9But Michael the archangel, when contending with the devil he disputed about the body of Moses, dared not bring against him a railing judgment, but said, The Lord rebuke you.*

When Michael and Satan were disputing over the body of Moses, Michael the archangel did not dare to bring a reviling accusation against Satan. The reason was that he recognized Satan, a cherub, as belonging to a higher order. He simply turned the matter of Moses' body over to the Lord, who was Satan's superior. But the fact that even the good archangel respected the fallen cherub shows that Satan is of the first rank. Satan is also the leader over all fallen angels, and not one of them is co-equal with him. That all fallen angels are under him is seen in Matthew 12:24 and Revelation 12:4, 7-8.

Fourth, Satan is a spirit being, just as all angelic or celestial beings are. This can be seen in Isaiah 14:12 ("day-star") and II Corinthians 11:14. He is consistently associated with angelic beings in Matthew 12:24 and Revelation 12:9.

Fifth, Satan is a confirmed sinner. The one verse that probably teaches this truth best is I John 3:8, which says that Satan has been sinning from the beginning. The fact that he is a confirmed sinner portrays exactly why he is pictured in the Bible as he is. His status is emphasized by Scripture in four ways:

1. Satan is characterized by ambitious pride (Ez. 28:17; I Tim. 3:6). The content of this pride is that he desired to be like God and that he was actually willing to lead a revolt in heaven.

2. He is characterized by untruths. According to John 8:44, Satan is the father of lies in that he was the first one to ever tell a lie. He is characterized as a liar himself.

3. He is characterized by craftiness that arises out of the crookedness of his very nature (II Cor. 2:11; 11:3-4; Eph. 6:11). He is a confirmed sinner down to his nature; there is a corruption of all that he is.

4. He is characterized by deceptiveness, which arises out of his craftiness (II Cor. 11:14; II Thess. 2:9-10). While the term "craftiness" deals with his actual nature, "deceptiveness" deals with his actions, which are a result of his craftiness.

Sixth, Satan is a performer of miracles. This part of his nature is seen in II Thessalonians 2:9, where Paul stated: *even he, whose coming is according to the working of Satan with all power and signs and lying wonders.* The Greek word for "working" is *energeian.* It means "efficiency," "the power with which error works." In the New Testament, the Greek term is used "only of superhuman power, whether of God or of the devil."[8] The implication is that the Antichrist will be energized by Satan with all the power and ability to perform tremendous miracles. Revelation 13:11-15 reveals this about Satan's miraculous powers:

> [11]*And I saw another beast coming up out of the earth; and he had two horns like unto a lamb, and he spoke as a dragon.* [12]*And he exercises all the authority of the first beast in his sight. And he makes the earth and them that dwell therein to worship the first beast, whose death-stroke was healed.* [13]*And he does great signs, that he should even make fire to come down out of heaven upon the earth in the sight of men.* [14]*And he deceives them that dwell on the earth by reason of the signs which it was given him to do in the sight of the beast; saying to them that dwell on the earth, that they should make an image to the beast who has the stroke of the sword and lived.* [15]*And it was given unto him to give breath to it, even to the image of*

---

[8] Strong's NT 1753; retrieved from https://biblehub.com/Greek/1753.htm.

the beast, that the image of the beast should both speak, and cause that as many as should not worship the image of the beast should be killed.

According to this passage, Satan will resurrect the Antichrist back to life. Furthermore, an image of the Antichrist will be set up in the temple in Jerusalem during the tribulation period, and through the power of Satan, this image becomes alive. So, Satan does have tremendous miraculous powers, even to the point of creating life (Ex. 7:11-12). This is why one must be very careful not to be convinced of the truth of something simply because of the existence of outward manifestations. Satan can duplicate a great number of miracles, some of which are found in Matthew 7:22-23:

[22]Many will say to me in that day, Lord, Lord, did we not prophesy by your name, and by your name cast out demons, and by your name do many mighty works? [23]And then will I profess unto them, I never knew you: depart from me, ye that work iniquity.

Because he has great miraculous powers, it is dangerous to underestimate Satan's abilities.

Seventh, Satan is a limited being. He does not have God's "omni" attributes. His widespread network of demons makes him appear to be omnipresent. His long experience in observing human responses to every trick and stimulus in every generation makes him appear to be omniscient. His power of miracles makes him appear to be omnipotent. Still, he possesses none of these attributes. Satan's limitations are determined by God. The best illustration of this is seen in Job 1-2, where God set the boundaries for Satan. God told him how far he could go and allowed him to go no further. Furthermore, Satan can be resisted (Eph. 6:10-18; Jas. 4:7; I Pet. 5:8-9). The fact that believers can resist him shows that Satan is a limited being.

F. Questions and Study Suggestions

Question 1: How many Old Testament books mention and teach the existence of Satan?

Question 2: How many New Testament books mention and teach the existence of Satan? How many NT writers mention Satan?

Question 3: How can you prove that Satan exists?

Question 4: What does it mean that Satan sealed up the sum (Ez. 28:11-12)?

Question 5: What type or category of angel is Satan?

Study Suggestion 1: Look up all the Gospel references given, read them, and make a brief note about each reference.

Study Suggestion 2: List the ten titles of Satan and reflect on what each title expresses either in regard to Satan's position or his character.

A Study of the Angelic Realm

Chapter III

The Fall of Satan

The fall of Satan is mentioned in four Bible passages. They will be detailed in this chapter, beginning with the key passage of Ezekiel 28:11-19. In these verses, Ezekiel addressed Satan by one of his many titles, king of Tyre. In the following phrase-by-phrase exposition, a distinction will be made between the prince of Tyre and the king of Tyre. Furthermore, the fall of the king of Tyre will be discussed. In the second part of this chapter, three other Scriptures will be detailed. These are I John 3:8, I Timothy 3:6, and Isaiah 14:12-14.

A. Ezekiel 28:11-19

Ezekiel 28:11-19 will be discussed in two parts. Verses 11-15 speak of the prince and the king of Tyre, and verses 16-19 deal with the fall of the king of Tyre.

1. The Prince of Tyre and the King of Tyre – Ezekiel 28:11-15

[11]Moreover the word of Jehovah came unto me, saying, [12]Son of man, take up a lamentation over the king of Tyre, and say unto him, Thus says the Lord Jehovah: You seal up the sum, full of wisdom, and perfect in beauty. [13]You were in Eden, the garden of God; every precious stone was your covering, the sardius, the topaz, and the diamond, the beryl, the onyx, and the jasper, the sapphire, the emerald, and the carbuncle, and gold: the workmanship of your tabrets and of your pipes was in you; in the day that you were

created they were prepared. ^{14}*You were the anointed cherub that covers; and I set you, so that you were upon the holy mountain of God; you have walked up and down in the midst of the stones of fire.* ^{15}*You were perfect in your ways from the day that you were created, till unrighteousness was found in you.*

a. The Prince of Tyre and the King of Tyre

There is an important connection between these verses and the previous prophecy of Ezekiel 28:1-10. In verse 2a, God said to Ezekiel: *Son of man, say unto the prince of Tyre, thus says the Lord Jehovah.* Ezekiel was to address an individual whom God called "the prince of Tyre." From the human perspective, this man was a king; but from the divine perspective, he is given the lesser title of prince. However, in verses 11-19, Ezekiel was dealing with "the king of Tyre." What is the relationship between the prince and the king of Tyre?

The human prince of Tyre was Ithobaal II, whose name also appears as Itto-Baal, Ethobaal, or Ethbaal. He was the Phoenician king of Tyre, who lived in the 8th century B.C. Not much is known about Ithobaal other than that he paid tribute to the Assyrian king Tiglath-pileser III in 738 B.C. and that he was able to control the sea lane traffic of the Mediterranean by virtue of his position. Because of this control, he gained a great deal of wealth, and with that wealth came power and authority.

God's judgement of the prince of Tyre is given in verse 2b: *Because your heart is lifted up, and you have said, I am a god, I sit in the seat of God, in the midst of the seas; yet you are man, and not God, though you did set your heart as the heart of God.* A day came in King Ithobaal's life that he was meditating in a wrongful manner upon his wealth, his power, and his authority, and he was filled with pride. This pride led to his self-declaration of deity. For this pride, he was condemned by God through Ezekiel. While the world called this individual the "king of Tyre," the real king of Tyre was not the visible person sitting on the throne, but an invisible being, Satan, who was controlling the visible one. The invisible being was the true king of Tyre, who once fell for the same reason: the problem of pride that led to a self-declaration of deity. Although verses 11-19 do not state that Satan also claimed to be god, there is a parallel passage, in which Satan declared: *I will make myself like the Most High* (Isa. 14:14).

So, the connection between the visible king, Ithobaal II, and the invisible king, Satan, was the problem of pride.

b. The Command to Lament the King of Tyre

Verses 11-12a contain a command by God to lament the king of Tyre. Ezekiel declared that *the word of Jehovah* came to him. This expression caused the prophet to turn his attention away from the visible prince of Tyre of verses 1-10 to the invisible king of Tyre, Satan. The expression also introduced three things: a new prophecy, a new individual, and a new title.

In verse 12a, Ezekiel was told to *take up a lamentation*. The Hebrew word for "lamentation," *qinah*, means "elegy" or "dirge." The Lord Jehovah Himself was proclaiming this lamentation. Although Satan had become a great sinner and led a rebellion against Him, God lamented over his fall. Ezekiel was to declare specific things concerning this new individual that could not be true of a mere human being.

c. The Description of the King of Tyre

The description of the king of Tyre is given in verses 12b-13. According to verse 12b, he *sealed up the sum* and was *full of wisdom* and *perfect in beauty*. The Hebrew word for "seal," *chatham*, means "to fill up" or "to complete." The picture is that, as God began to do His work of creation, He chose to limit Himself to a specific blueprint or pattern and willed not to go beyond that. When angels were created, they filled up only so much of this pattern. Animals filled it up some more. Man filled it up even more. The expression "to seal up the sum," then, means "to fill up a pattern" or "to fill up a blueprint." In his original state, this king of Tyre, meaning Satan, was created in such a way that he filled up the entire pattern in two areas: First, he was full of wisdom, meaning he was the wisest of all created beings; second, he was perfect in beauty, meaning he was the most beautiful of all created beings. Throughout the centuries, the tendency of artists has been to portray Satan as an ugly or hideous creature, but that is not the picture the Scriptures draw. In fact, just the opposite is true. Of all created beings, Satan is both the most beautiful and the wisest. When dealing with this being in spiritual warfare, it is important for believers to recognize him for what he is. In his outward form, he was created perfect in beauty, and in the mental realm, he was created with perfection of wisdom. Verse 12b describes Satan during his time in his first abode, which was the throne of God. As will be seen in the next chapter, in his "career," Satan's abode undergoes six changes in chronological sequence. His first two abodes are now past history; his third abode is where he currently functions; and his fourth, fifth, and sixth abodes are future.

In verse 13, Ezekiel made several statements about Satan's second abode, *Eden, the garden of God*. This was not the vegetable garden of Eden of the book of Genesis, but a mineral garden. In fact, it was the earth as it was originally created, a beautiful mineral garden, covered by various precious stones. There were no oceans and no seas. Furthermore, in this verse, God said to Satan: *every precious stone was your covering*. The Hebrew word for "covering," *mesukkah*, means "canopy." In other words, every precious stone served as a canopy over the king of Tyre. In summary, it should be noted that these precious stone served a dual purpose: They covered the king of Tyre, meaning Satan, as a canopy; and they covered the earth of Genesis 1:1 so that Satan was able to walk *up and down in the midst of the stones of fire* (v. 14).

Altogether there are ten stones listed in verse 13, and they are arranged in three sets of three, plus one precious metal. These stones and their alignment are almost identical to three of the four rows of stones on the breastplate of the high priest, as described in Exodus 28:17-20. The first set is *the sardius, the topaz, and the diamond*. This corresponds to the first row of stones on the breastplate of the high priest (Ex. 28:17), with one variation: In place of the diamond, there was the carbuncle. The second set is *the beryl, the onyx, and the jasper*. This corresponds to the fourth row of stones on the breastplate of the high priest (Ex. 28:20). The third set is *the sapphire, the emerald, and the carbuncle*. This corresponds to the second row of the breastplate of the high priest (Ex. 28:18), with the variation that in place of the carbuncle, there was the diamond. Finally, the tenth element in Satan's covering was *gold*, the one precious metal.

Summarizing the differences between what is described in Exodus and what is described in Ezekiel, the following points may be made: While in Exodus the stones were on the breastplate of the high priest, for the king of Tyre, they served as a canopy. Furthermore, the high priest had twelve stones, not ten. Yet, the similarity of what is described in these passages may imply that the king of Tyre had specific priestly functions in heaven corresponding to the function of the priest on earth, which was to represent men to God. The Scriptures make it clear that there is a Tabernacle in heaven, because the earthly Tabernacle was a copy of the heavenly one (Ex. 25:9, 40; 26:30; Heb. 8:2, 5; 9:11, 24). So, one of the functions of Satan may have been to represent all other angelic beings before God in the heavenly Tabernacle.

Verse 13 goes on to speak about Satan's activities in heaven: *the workmanship of your tabrets* [tambourines] *and of your pipes was in you*. The words "tabrets" and "pipes" could have two different meanings. They may refer to musical instruments. If this is their meaning, it implies that the king of Tyre led in divine worship. It would also give further credence to the statement made before that Satan may have served as the heavenly high priest leading in worship as well as being a priestly representative. The second possibility is that these words could refer to settings and sockets. If this is their meaning, it refers to the settings of the ten gems that were just mentioned. Normally, if a verse can be translated in two different ways, the context determines which way to go. But in this case, the context allows for a combination of both. The words "tabrets" and "pipes" refer to the gems and to their significance as well as to the fact that Satan led in priestly worship in heaven.

Finally, verse 13 ends by stating: *in the day that you were created they were prepared*. This part of the verse is one of several reasons to believe that Ezekiel was not speaking of the literal king of Tyre, Ithobaal II, but of Satan. The literal human king of Tyre was born, not created. Satan, on the other hand, was a created being. The phrase "they were prepared" refers to everything that was mentioned before, namely, his perfection in that he filled up the sum in wisdom and beauty, the canopy of stones, the musical instruments he could use to lead in worship, and his appointment as high priest in the heavenly Tabernacle. These are the things that were prepared for him or assigned to him in the day he was created.

d. The Position of the King of Tyre

In verse 14, Ezekiel made three statements about the position of Satan. First, Satan was *the anointed cherub that covers* (v. 14a). As a cherub, Satan is a member of the highest order of created beings (see Chapter I). The cherubim carry the Shechinah glory, so they are closest to the throne of God. While the angels are before the throne and the seraphim surround it, the cherubim are under the throne and are responsible for carrying it. The closer a being is to the throne, the higher his rank. Not only is Satan a cherub, he was also the *anointed* cherub. The Hebrew word for "anointed," *mimshach*, shares the same root as the Hebrew word for "Messiah."[9] So, Satan was the "messiahed" cherub. He was already first in beauty and wisdom. As a cherub, he was of the highest order of celestial beings. But he was one among many cherubim and was co-equal with them in power and authority. Yet, according to this verse, at some point in eternity past, God selected this particular cherub and "messiahed" him. This anointing gave Satan a position of authority and power that was above the other cherubim. He became the archcherub. As such, Satan was the one *that covers*. The Hebrew word for "covers," *cakak*, means "to overshadow," "to screen," "to cover something like a canopy." Satan was a canopy over the throne of God. While other cherubim were underneath the throne and were carrying the throne, he served as a canopy over the throne. This position made him the most prominent cherub of them all.

The second statement regarding Satan's position refers to the archcherub's first abode. The one making the statement is God, and He said, *I set you, so that you were upon the holy mountain of God* (v. 14b). The expression "I set you" means that this was a position given by God as a gift. God set Satan upon His holy mountain. The word "holy" emphasizes the nature of the place. But what is the mountain? The Bible uses many symbols, and whenever it does, it is consistent in its usage. Any one specific symbol will mean the same thing throughout the Scriptures in 95 percent of the cases. Whenever the word "mountain" is used

---

[9] Robert D. D. Jamieson, A.R. Fausset, David Brown, "Commentary on Ezekiel 28:14," *Commentary Critical and Explanatory on the Whole Bible – Unabridged*, accessed via www.studylight.org/commentaries/jfu/ezekiel-28.html.

symbolically, it is always the symbol of a king, a kingdom, or a throne. The holy mountain of God is the very throne of God itself, described in Ezekiel 1:26-28. At one time, Satan was a canopy over the very throne of God. That gave him a unique position. It meant that he served as the guardian of God's throne so that he controlled who among the other angelic beings had access to God and who among them did not. His first abode, then, was over the very throne of God.

The third statement describes Satan's position during his time in his second abode: *you have walked up and down in the midst of the stones of fire* (v. 14c). The expression "walked up and down" means "to walk to and fro." It is a very common figure used of satanic activity (Job 1:7; 2:2). It is also used of good angels and typifies angelic activity (Zech. 1:10-11; 6:7). Again, this describes the original earth of Genesis 1:1, which served as Satan's second abode. The stones of fire refer to the ten stones listed in verse 13 that covered the earth's surface before Satan's fall.

e. The Perfection of the King of Tyre

Verse 15 speaks about the perfection of the king of Tyre: *You were perfect in your ways from the day that you were created, till unrighteousness was found in you.* This verse makes three points about Satan. First, he was perfect in all his ways. The word "perfect" means that he was without any flaws. When God created Satan, he had no flaws whatsoever; he was perfect in his being. The expression "in your ways" emphasizes that his actions were as perfect as his being. He was flawless in his being and perfect in his activity for a specific, but unknown period of time.

Second, Satan was perfect from the day he was created. This is the second time Ezekiel noted that the king of Tyre was a created being. The fact that this king was created and the fact that he was the anointed cherub rule out that he was a mere human being. Furthermore, from the day that God created him, he was created perfect. This shows that the fault of Satan's fall did not lie with God, because the corruption of his person and actions came subsequent to his creation.

Third, Satan was perfect until unrighteousness was found in him. This is the closest the Bible comes to describing the origin of sin. One day, there it was! Satan was perfect in all of his ways, in his being, and in his actions, until at some point unrighteousness was found in him. The

Hebrew word for "unrighteousness," *evel* or *avlah*, means "injustice," "wrongdoings." This is the transition that led to the fall of Satan. The perfection of his ways or deeds eventually gave way to imperfection and wrongdoings. The fact that his deeds and actions became wrong presupposes a corruption of his person beforehand, because the corruption of a person always precedes the corruption of deeds.

2. The Fall of the King of Tyre – Ezekiel 28:16-19

16By the abundance of your traffic they filled the midst of you with violence, and you have sinned: therefore have I cast you as profane out of the mountain of God; and I have destroyed you, O covering cherub, from the midst of the stones of fire. 17Your heart was lifted up because of your beauty; you have corrupted your wisdom by reason of your brightness: I have cast you to the ground; I have laid you before kings, that they may behold you. 18By the multitude of your iniquities, in the unrighteousness of your traffic, you have profaned your sanctuaries; therefore have I brought forth a fire from the midst of you; it has devoured you, and I have turned you to ashes upon the earth in the sight of all them that behold you. 19All they that know you among the peoples shall be astonished at you: you are become a terror, and you shall nevermore have any being.

a. The Corruption and Judgment of Satan

In verse 16a, Ezekiel spelled out the content of Satan's sinful deeds, making three points. First, Satan committed sin "by the abundance of his traffic." The same figure was used of the human prince of Tyre, Ithobaal II, in Ezekiel 28:1-10. For him, it meant that he went from port to port gathering wealth (Ez. 28:5). But for the king of Tyre, Satan, it meant going from angel to angel slandering God in order to win their allegiance. Eventually, he convinced one-third of all the angels that God was in the wrong (Rev. 12:4). Because he originated lying, Satan became the father of lies (Jn. 8:44). The corruption of his being led to his wrong deeds, which was lying about God.

Second, the verse states: *they filled the midst of you with violence.* The phrase "they filled" refers to the trafficking from angel to angel, bad-mouthing God. This evil deed led to violence because it meant that Satan led a revolt against God's authority in heaven. Furthermore, this act began a conflict between good angels and fallen angels that continues to this day and will continue until the middle of the tribulation, at which point Satan will be cast out of heaven to his fourth abode, the earth (Rev. 12:7-12).

Third, the verse declares, *you have sinned*. The Hebrew word for "sinned," *watteḥĕṭā* (*wattecheta*), means that Satan missed the mark. As a result of his actions, he missed the mark of his high calling. Thus, Satan became the first sinner in the angelic realm. While Eve was the first sinner in the human sphere, Satan's sin preceded Eve's sin.

As a consequence of Satan's wrongdoings, God pronounced two aspects of judgment in verse 16b. First, the perfect cherub became the profane cherub. God stated: *Therefore have I cast you as profane out of the mountain of God*. Because of his wrongdoings, Satan lost the high position of his first abode, the mountain of God, and was no longer the guardian of God's throne. Second, God stated: *I have destroyed you, O covering cherub, from the midst of the stones of fire*. This refers to the loss of Satan's position in his second abode, when he lost his authority over planet earth. The word "destroyed" does not mean he was destroyed in his being, but that he was destroyed from his position in Eden, the garden of God. Through man's fall, Satan was able to usurp man's authority over the earth. To this day, he remains the prince of this world (Jn. 14:30) and the god of this age (II Cor. 4:4). However, his rightful authority ceased when he was destroyed from the midst of the stones of fire. The phrase "I have destroyed you, O covering cherub" points out the loss of Satan's position and priestly worship functions.

Verse 17 deals with the corruption of Satan's being and its consequences. The corruption of his being is described in verse 17a: *Your heart was lifted up because of your beauty; you have corrupted your wisdom by reason of your brightness*. Satan looked upon his beauty in a wrong manner. Rather than remaining in humble submission to God, who made him that way, he allowed pride to set in.

While the first sinner was Satan, the first sin was pride. This comes out clearly in the context of I Timothy 3:6, where Paul outlined a series of qualifications for anyone who would desire to become an elder in a local church. A *novice*, meaning a new believer, may not be given a position of authority, *lest being puffed up he fall into the condemnation of the devil.* It is clear from this verse that Satan was filled with pride. That is the sin that corrupted his being and led to the wrong deeds.

Furthermore, Satan corrupted his wisdom by reason of his brightness. He looked upon his beauty in a wrong way, and this act led to the sin of pride. The sin of pride, in turn, corrupted his perfect wisdom, which was first mentioned in verse 12. Since his fall, Satan has used his great wisdom for sinful purposes. Many ask the question, "If Satan knows the Bible and knows what is going to happen to him in the end, why is he still trying to fight against it all?" The answer lies right here. Although his wisdom was so great, it has been corrupted by sin, and to some degree, he feels he can still win.

As the consequence of the corruption of Satan's being, God pronounced judgment in verse 17b and made two statements concerning the punishment He decreed for Satan. First, He stated: *I have cast you to the ground.* This might be a summary of the loss of Satan's first two abodes, mentioned earlier in the passage. However, it might also be what is known as a "prophetic perfect," in which a future event is stated in the past tense. If it is a prophetic perfect, it describes Satan's fall from his third abode to his fourth abode. Today, Satan is dwelling in his third abode, the atmospheric heavens. According to Revelation 12:7-12, in the middle of the tribulation, he will be cast out of the atmospheric heavens down to the earth, where he will be confined for the second half of the tribulation. That will be his fourth abode, where he will live for 3½ years. Second, God stated: *I have laid you before kings, that they may behold you.* This sentence is important in that it supports the concept of a prophetic perfect. At the time of Satan's fall, there were no human kings. Satan fell before Adam and Eve were even created. So, this is clearly a prophetic perfect and a reference to Satan's fifth and sixth abodes, the abyss (Rev 20:1-3) and the lake of fire (Rev 20:7-10). In both locations, there will be kings who will look at Satan in amazement.

Verse 18 provides a detailed description of Satan's sinful deeds and the consequence of these deeds, beginning in verse 18a with the description: *By the multitude of your iniquities, in the unrighteousness of your traffic, you have profaned your sanctuaries.* The word "iniquities" refers to

Satan's internal corruption and is the third term used for sin in this passage. The one sin of pride led to a multitude of corruptions of Satan's character. Furthermore, in this verse, the word "unrighteousness" means "vanity." The word "traffic" refers to Satan's going from angel to angel slandering God. The corruption of Satan's character led to deeds of corruption. He corrupted other celestial beings so that one-third of all angels fell with him. Lastly, the verse points out that Satan profaned his own sanctuaries. The word "sanctuaries" refers to the holy places of heaven. It is in the plural because the heavenly Tabernacle has both a holy place and a holy of holies. Satan once had a priestly function in the Tabernacle in heaven. As the high priest, he led the worship in the heavenly sanctuaries before his fall. By performing sinful deeds in heaven, Satan brought corruption to heaven. Therefore, Hebrews 9:23-26 states that the heavenly sanctuaries needed to be cleaned by the blood of the Messiah. Yeshua took His blood into heaven after His resurrection. This is the reason Mary Magdalene could not touch Him (Jn. 20:17). Only after He had cleansed the heavenly Tabernacle was He touchable.

As a consequence of Satan's sinful deeds, God pronounced judgment, in verse 18b: *Therefore have I brought forth a fire from the midst of you; it has devoured you, and I have turned you to ashes upon the earth in the sight of all them that behold you.* The word "therefore" connects the judgment with Satan's sinful deeds of verse 18a. God made three statements concerning the consequences. First, He brought forth a fire from the midst of Satan. At one time, this fire was a mark of Satan's glory. Now, it would be used to punish him. This prophecy will be fulfilled when Satan is confined in his sixth abode, the lake of fire. The principle is that unless there is repentance and confession, sin always carries within itself the seeds of its own destruction. Second, God declared that the fire has devoured Satan. He made this statement as a prophetic perfect, speaking of Satan's demise in the lake of fire. Third, God stated that He has turned Satan to ashes upon the earth in the sight of all who beheld him. Insofar as the earth is concerned, Satan will be nothing more than ashes when he is confined in his last two abodes. Unsaved people will see him in the fifth abode, the abyss (Rev. 20:1-3), and they will see him in the sixth abode, the lake of fire (Rev. 20:7-10).

b. The Results of Satan's Fall

The results of Satan's fall are given in verse 19: *All they that know you among the peoples shall be astonished at you: you are become a terror, and you shall nevermore have any being.* The verse makes three points. First, all who knew Satan will be surprised by his demise. The word "all" includes the fallen angels and his many followers among humanity. They thought that he would be their leader, their savior, their victor over God Himself. He will prove to be a failure, and this will astonish them.

Second, Satan has become a terror. In Hebrew, the word for "terror" is in the plural, emphasizing the intensity of terror. Satan's fall has greatly intensified terror, and it will intensify terror even more for those who followed him because if their leader has been sentenced to the lake of fire, what chance do they have of escaping the same fate? They will be filled with many terrors as a result of Satan's demise in his sixth abode.

Third, he will have no more being. The Hebrew literally reads "Unto you nothing for a long time or forever." As an eternal creature, Satan will always exist, but he will no longer exist on this earth, and he will no longer be active. He will be forever and ever in the lake of fire. In that sense, he shall not be anymore.

B. Other Verses Detailing Satan's Fall

The fall of Satan is described in three other passages of Scripture, the first one being I John 3:8: *he that does sin is of the devil; for the devil sins from the beginning. To this end was the Son of God manifested, that he might destroy the works of the devil.* The point of this verse is that Satan was the first sinner.

The second passage is I Timothy 3:6: *not a novice, lest being puffed up he fall into the condemnation of the devil.* In the previous discussion of this verse, it was pointed out that in its context is the question of leadership. Paul listed a series of qualifications for anyone who would like to become an elder in a local church. He stated that a new believer must never be placed in a position of authority. By virtue of the fact that he is a new believer, he is spiritually immature. If he were to be placed in a position of leadership before he is spiritually ready for it, he might be filled with pride, which could cause him to fall into the same sin that caused Satan's fall. The first sin, then, was the sin of pride.

The third passage on Satan's fall is Isaiah 14:12-14:

[12]How are you fallen from heaven, O day-star, son of the morning! how are you cut down to the ground, that did lay low the nations! [13]And you said in your heart, I will ascend into heaven, I will exalt my throne above the stars of God; and I will sit upon the mount of congregation, in the uttermost parts of the north; [14]I will ascend above the heights of the clouds; I will make myself like the Most High.

In some translations, the term "day-star" is replaced with the name Lucifer, and there has been a discussion about this name in a previous section of this book. Of importance here is that Isaiah referred to Satan as the "day-star" and "the son of the morning," who, at some point, fell. This is followed by Satan's five "I will" statements that were the reason for his fall (vv. 13-14). He uttered them when he was filled with pride. The content of Satan's sin is reflected in these five "I will" statements, and each exclamation has a specific significance.

First, he said, "I will ascend into heaven." He was not satisfied with the very high position God had already given him as the guardian of His throne and with authority over the mineral garden of Eden. He desired a higher position, a higher estate than he already had. There was no higher position than God's throne. With this first "I will," he declared a desire to usurp God's authority. Instead of being the one overshadowing the throne, he now wished to become the throne-sitter.

Second, he declared, "I will exalt my throne above the stars of God." Normally, whenever the word "star" is used symbolically in the Scriptures, it represents angels. With the second "I will," Satan declared his desire to become the sole authority over all the angels that God had created. By so doing, he intended to depose Michael from his position and become the archangel.

Third, he said, "I will sit on the mount of the congregation, on the farthest sides of the north." The Hebrew prophets used these expressions in describing the Messianic kingdom. Satan knew God's program quite well and understood that the Messiah will rule over the nation of Israel during the millennium. Hence, with this third "I will," he declared his desire to make himself the messianic ruler over Israel.

Fourth, he said, "I will ascend above the heights of the clouds." Whenever the word "cloud" is used symbolically, it is always a symbol of God's unique Shechinah glory. It is a glory that belongs to God alone and something which Satan desired for himself.

Fifth, he declared, "I will make myself like the Most High." According to Genesis 14:18-20, whenever God is referred to by the title "Most High," it emphasizes that He owns the heavens and the earth. With this fifth "I will," Satan declared his desire to become the sole possessor of all that God created in the first verse of Genesis.

These five "I wills" resulted from the pride of Satan and caused him to lead a revolt against God in which he was followed by one-third of the angelic host (Rev. 12:3-4). In this way, the day-star, son of the morning, became Satan the adversary. At that point, judgment came upon him.

It is interesting to note that in the Ezekiel 28 passage dealing with the origin and fall of Satan, the prelude to the discussion is Ezekiel's condemnation of the prince of Tyre (vv. 1-10). According to verses 2 and 6-9, the sin of the prince of Tyre was his desire to be like God. The description of this sin is the background to the sin of the king of Tyre, who was Satan and who desired to be like God (Ez. 28:11-19). The desire to be like God was the satanic motive that caused the fall of Satan. According to Genesis 3:5, the desire to be like God was also the sin that caused the fall of man. The context of this verse presents Satan's second attack on man, where he moved from questioning what God said to an outward negation of God's words. It begins in verse 4 with a denial of the penalty: *And the serpent said unto the woman, You shall not surely die*. Here is the first lie of Scripture, and it is the reason why Yeshua called Satan the father of lies (Jn. 8:44). Satan moved from a perverted question to an outward denial. In verse 5, he moved from a denial of the penalty to a denial of God's integrity: *for God does know that in the day ye eat thereof, then your eyes shall be opened, and ye shall be as God, knowing good and evil*. Satan wanted to create in Eve the desire to be like God, and this second attack on man was successful. Eve did indeed develop this desire and thus reflected the mind of Satan.

The greatest reflection of the satanic mind and the satanic motive is yet to come. The major sin of the Antichrist will be that same desire to be like God. This can be seen in II Thessalonians 2:4, which states that the son of perdition will oppose and exalt *himself against all that is called God or that is worshipped; so that he sits in the temple of God, setting himself forth as God.* Any desire to be like God is to reflect the mind of Satan. In contrast, the mind of the Messiah is seen in Philippians 2:5-11:

> *⁵Have this mind in you, which was also in Messiah Yeshua: ⁶who, existing in the form of God, counted not the being on an equality with God a thing to be grasped, ⁷but emptied himself, taking the form of a servant, being made in the likeness of men; ⁸and being found in fashion as a man, he humbled himself, becoming obedient even unto death, yea, the death of the cross. ⁹Wherefore also God highly exalted him, and gave unto him the name which is above every name; ¹⁰that in the name of Yeshua every knee should bow, of things in heaven and things on earth and things under the earth, ¹¹and that every tongue should confess that Yeshua Messiah is Lord, to the glory of God the Father.*

To have the mind of the Messiah is to be like a servant. The believer who desires to be a servant and will take a servant's role is reflecting the mind of the Messiah.

C. Questions and Study Suggestions

Question 1: If someone were to ask you which verses speak of Satan's fall, what would your answer be?

Question 2: When did Satan fall? Support your answer with the proper verses.

Question 3: Why did Satan fall?

Question 4: What did Yeshua mean when He said, "I saw Satan fall like lightning from heaven" (Lk. 10:18, NKJV)?

Study Suggestion 1: List Satan's "I will" statements and God's response to the underlying sin as described in Ezekiel 28:16.

Chapter IV

The Six Abodes of Satan

The Scriptures clearly teach that Satan has a "career." However, this career is rarely traced from start to finish. One of the better ways of tracing the course of Satan's life is by means of the six abodes in which he either has lived in the past (the first two), is living in the present (the third), or will live in the future (the fourth, fifth, and sixth).

Some of what will be stated in the next few paragraphs has been mentioned in previous chapters of this book. However, the understanding of the six abodes of Satan is vital to an understanding of the position of the believer in spiritual warfare. Therefore, some repetition may be important to underscore the flow of the chronology of Satan's career.

A. The First Abode: The Throne of God

The first abode of Satan is given in Ezekiel 28:14 as being *upon the holy mountain of God*. The Bible is very consistent in its usage of symbols. A specific symbol will mean the same thing throughout the Old and New Testaments in about 95 percent of the cases. For example, whenever the word "stone" is used symbolically, it always represents the second Person of the Trinity, God the Son. Whenever the word "mountain" is used symbolically, it always stands for a king, kingdom, or throne. Both of these symbols are found together in a very famous prophetic passage, in Daniel 2. Nebuchadnezzar dreamed of a huge image composed of various metals which Daniel interpreted to represent the times of the Gentiles, an era when the Gentiles will have domination over the Jewish people. In his dream, Nebuchadnezzar then saw a small stone that *smote the image upon its feet that were of iron and clay, and broke them in pieces* (v. 34). Daniel interpreted this to represent the second coming, when Yeshua the Messiah will return and smash Gentile domination over the Jewish people. In the dream, the stone began to grow and grow until it became a huge mountain that filled the entire earth (v. 35). Daniel interpreted the mountain as representing the millennial kingdom, in which the Messiah will rule over the entire world. Again, the Scriptures do use many symbols, but they are consistent in the usage of these symbols. Thus, Satan's first abode is described in Ezekiel 28:14 as being *upon the holy mountain of God*, meaning that he was over the throne of God, as a canopy overshadowing it. Other details of Satan in his first abode were discussed previously.

B. The Second Abode: The Mineral Garden of Eden

Satan's second abode is described in verse 13 of Ezekiel 28: *You were in Eden, the garden of God*. After creating angelic beings (Job 38:4-7), God created the heavens and the earth (Gen. 1:1). Different parts of the universe were given over to the authority of different angelic beings. Earth was assigned to Satan. The garden of Eden of Ezekiel 28:13 was not the same as the garden of Genesis 2-3. The latter was a vegetable garden, but the former is described as a mineral garden. According to Ezekiel 28:13, when our planet was originally created, it had no oceans or seas and was covered with the brightness of the precious stones mentioned in this verse. These stones exuded light and so are called "the stones of fire" in verse 14. Satan was able to walk up and down in the midst of these stones. The Hebrew verb for "walk up and down" really means "to walk to and fro," which is a common figure used by the Scriptures of satanic activity (Job 1:7; 2:2). However, it is also used of good angels and therefore typifies angelic activity in general (Zech. 1:10-11; 6:7). So, Satan walked up and down, to and fro, in the midst of the stones of fire. This planet, entirely in the form of a mineral garden, served as Satan's second abode for an unknown period before any human being was created.

Verse 13 also states that every precious stone was Satan's covering. The Hebrew word for "covering" means "canopy." In other words, these stones, that according to the subsequent verse covered the whole earth, also served as a canopy over Satan. Thus, they had a double purpose.

Ten stones are listed as three sets of three, plus one. The first set consists of the sardius, the topaz, and the diamond. The second set encompasses the beryl, the onyx, and the jasper. Third is the sapphire, the emerald, and the carbuncle. The one single element is gold, which is a precious metal rather than a precious stone.

Many of the stones mentioned in Ezekiel 28 are the same as the stones of the breastplate of the Jewish high priest, and this is significant. The following table shows the precious stones listed in Ezekiel 28 and compares them with those mentioned in Exodus 28 in connection with the high priestly breastplate. The differences in the gems are highlighted in gray.

Ezekiel 28:13	Group	Exodus 28:17-20	Row
Sardius	#1	Sardius	#1 (v. 17)
Topaz		Topaz	
Diamond		Carbuncle	
Beryl	#2	Beryl	#4 (v. 20)
Onyx		Onyx	
Jasper		Jasper	
Sapphire	#3	Sapphire	#2 (v. 18)
Emerald		Emerald	
Carbuncle		Diamond	
Gold		Gold	
		Jacinth	#3 (v. 19)
		Agate	
		Amethyst	

To summarize the differences, while the stones were on the breastplate of the high priest, for Satan, they served as a canopy. Furthermore, the high priest had twelve and not ten stones. However, despite the differences, the mention of the precious stones in the canopy of Satan may indicate that he had specific priestly functions in heaven before his fall. He may have served as a priest in heaven. There is a Tabernacle in heaven, and the earthly Tabernacle was a copy of it. From Ezekiel 28:13-14, it appears that Satan was the heavenly high priest. Of course, since his fall, he no longer serves in that capacity. Today, Yeshua is our High Priest.

Verse 13 goes on to state: *the workmanship of your tabrets and of your pipes was in you*. In the previous discussion of the verse, it has become clear that the context allows for the words "tabrets" and "pipes" to refer to two things. On the one hand, they may refer to the musical instruments that Satan used to lead in worship. On the other hand, the phrase may also be translated as "of your settings and of your sockets." Then, the expression would refer to the settings of the precious stones that were mentioned in the same verse. The actual meaning of the Hebrew terms tends to indicate musical instruments, but contextually, both readings are possible. The verse may even be understood as a combination of both renderings, referring to the gems and to the significance of the gems: Satan led in priestly worship in heaven.

Finally, the verse states: *in the day that you were created they were prepared*. Again, Ezekiel repeated that the being he spoke of was created. That which was assigned to this creature included those things which were spoken of: his perfection (he filled up the sum in wisdom and beauty), the canopy of precious stones, and the musical instruments by which he could lead in worship. On the day that he was created, Satan was already the appointed high priest, to function in the heavenly Tabernacle.

While Satan was in his second abode, he fell. The event is described in Ezekiel 28:16-19 and was discussed in detail in the previous chapter of this book. In summary, God decreed the twofold punishment of Satan, saying in verse 17b: *I have cast you to the ground; I have laid you before kings, that they may behold you*. First, He declared that He has cast Satan to the ground. This punishment might be a summary of the loss of Satan's first two abodes, mentioned earlier in the passage. However, it might also be what is known as a prophetic perfect, in which a future event is stated as a past act. If it is a prophetic perfect, then it describes Satan's fall from the third abode to his fourth abode. Second, God declared that He made a spectacle of Satan before kings. This did not happen at the time of Satan's fall, because no kings existed. In fact, he fell even before Adam and Eve were created. Hence, the statement is a prophetic perfect and a reference to Satan's last two abodes, where Satan will indeed be beheld by kings.

Verse 18b deals further with the punishment, and God states, *Therefore have I brought forth a fire from the midst of you; it has devoured you, and I have turned you to ashes upon the earth in the sight of all them that behold you.* "Therefore," that is, because of verse 18a, three things come by way of punishment. First, God brought fire from Satan's midst. At one time, this fire was a mark of Satan's glory, as the stones of fire beautified him. Now, fire will be used to punish him. This will be fulfilled when he is confined in his sixth abode, the lake of fire. As mentioned before, the principle is that sin always carries within itself the seeds of its own destruction, and it will destroy the one performing the sin unless there is repentance and confession. Second, this fire has devoured Satan. The verb is in the prophetic perfect, thus referring to the lake of fire. Third, God will turn Satan to ashes upon the earth in the sight of all who saw him. Insofar as the earth is concerned, the fallen cherub will be ashes; he will be nothing when he will be confined in his last two abodes. As mentioned in the previous paragraph, he will be beheld by many in the abyss and in the lake of fire.

Finally, verse 19 gives the three results, stating: *All they that know you among the peoples shall be astonished at you: you are become a terror, and you shall nevermore have any being.* The first result of God's punishment of Satan is that all who knew him will be astonished at him because of his demise. The "all" includes the angels who followed him in his revolt as well as the many followers he has had among humanity. They thought that he would be their leader, their savior, their victor over God Himself. He will prove to be a failure, and this will astonish them. Second, the verse declares that he has become a terror. In the Hebrew text, the word for "terror," *ballahah*, is in the plural, emphasizing the intensity of horror. He has greatly intensified terror, but his fall will intensify horror even more because if the leader has been sentenced to the lake of fire, how much truer will this be for his followers? They will be filled with many terrors as a result of Satan's demise in the lake of fire. Third, God declares that Satan shall be no more forever. The Hebrew literally reads, "unto you nothing for a long time (or forever)." Of course, Satan shall always be. He is an eternal being, and he will always exist. But the point is that he will no longer exist on this earth, and he will no longer be active. He will be forever and ever in the lake of fire. In that sense, he shall nevermore have any being.

When God judged Satan, He also judged everything under Satan's authority, including the original earth, the mineral garden of Eden. The conditions of Genesis 1:2 came into being as a result of this judgment. The earth became waste and void, although it was not originally created that way (Is. 45:18). The beautiful mineral garden that the planet once was became totally covered by oceans. Some time after this judgment came the six days of creation, recorded in Genesis 1. The oceans were partially removed to allow dry land to appear, but the effects of Satan's judgment are still here in that most of the earth is still covered by oceans. The effects of the fall of Satan will not be fully removed until the creation of the new heavens and the new earth, which will not have any oceans (Rev. 21:1). The new earth will be covered with the same type of precious stones that this planet was once covered with before the fall of Satan. In other words, the new earth, which will be the eternal abode of all believers, will look as this planet first looked when it was originally created.[10]

This author places the fall of Satan between Genesis 1:1 and 1:2. This position is often referred to as the "gap theory." But many people who hold to the gap theory do so in order to allow for the existence of dinosaurs. They attempt to fit the fossil and geological ages into the gap and are forced to make the gap millions of years long. They adapt their biblical interpretation to certain scientific theories. However, this is not the position of the author, since, scripturally, it would be impossible for death to

---

[10] Most Hebrew scholars agree that Genesis 1:2 describes a chaotic state. The issue of the creation account boils down to the question: Did God create the universe in a chaotic state and then brought order to it or did some event cause it to become chaotic? This author prefers the second option because of Isaiah 45:18 and because terms used in Genesis 1:2 are used elsewhere in the Hebrew text to describe divine judgments. Also, the new earth in Revelation 21:1-22:5 compares favorably with Ezekiel 28:13, showing that the new earth will look much like the old earth prior to the covering by seas in Genesis 1:2.

exist before the fall of man (Rom. 5:12). Thus, all fossils and mammoth creatures have coexisted with man rather than preceded man. There is a gap between Genesis 1:1 and 1:2 only for the fall of Satan, and this need not be a very long time at all.

On the sixth day of creation, God created man and gave him the authority over the earth which had been revoked from Satan. But when man fell, Satan usurped authority over the earth, setting the stage for his activities in his third abode.

C. The Third Abode: The Atmospheric Heavens

The third and present abode of Satan is disclosed in Ephesians 2:2 and 6:12:

✧ Ephesians 2:2: *Wherein ye once walked according to the course of this world, according to the prince of the powers of the air, of the spirit that now works in the sons of disobedience.*

✧ Ephesians 6:2: *For our wrestling is not against flesh and blood, but against the principalities, against the powers, against the world-rulers of this darkness, against the spiritual hosts of wickedness in the heavenly places.*

The first verse describes Satan as the prince of the powers of the air, while the second describes him as existing in the heavenly places. Accordingly, Satan's third abode can be labeled as the atmospheric heavens. He lives in the air or atmosphere.

While the atmospheric heavens function as his third and present abode, Satan has permission to access two other places. First, he has access into heaven and often uses it for the purpose of accusing the brethren. He functioned that way in the life of Job (Job 1:6; 2:1) and continues to do so in the case of many believers today (Rev. 12:10), and also in the case of the nation of Israel (Zech. 3:1). Second, Satan has permission for access to the earth and uses it frequently as well. As a result of Adam's fall, he is now the prince of this world (Jn. 12:31), the god of this age (II Cor. 4:4), and can offer the kingdoms of this world to whomever he wills (Lk. 4:5-7).

When Satan comes to the earth, it is in one of two forms. The first form is that of a roaring lion (I Pet. 5:8). In this form, his basic aim is to devour and destroy. This is the way he often appeared to Israel; all anti-Semitic campaigns throughout Jewish history have been instigated by Satan as the roaring lion. Also, he has often appeared to the church in this form, and many of the persecutions against the church have been inspired by Satan as the roaring lion. Satan works on the principle that whomsoever the Lord loves, he will hate. God, throughout the Prophets and the New Testament, spelled out His eternal love for the people of Israel; therefore, Satan has had a perpetual war against the Jews, seeking to destroy them at every possible opportunity.

The second form in which Satan appears when he comes to the earth is as an angel of light (II Cor. 11:14). In this form, his basic aim is to deceive. It is the ultimate carrying out of the fifth "I will" of Isaiah 14:12-14, the "I will make myself like the Most High." Even Satan knew he could not *be* God, so he decided to become just *like* the Most High. By instigating a counterfeit program that often looks like the real thing, he has been able to implement a work of deception even among true believers, encouraging them to focus on experience and blinding them to their need for careful study of the Word of God. The program of deception is carried out against both believers (II Cor. 11:3) and unbelievers (Rev. 20:3).

The nature of a counterfeit is to look like the original. Counterfeit money, for example, is not obviously fake money. It looks so much like real money that it is hard to detect the differences. It takes training to be able to differentiate between the real thing and its counterfeit. However, counterfeit money does tend to have flaws. Perhaps the wrong type of paper is used, the wrong type of ink, or the wrong design in some obscure corner of the bill. Yet, the flaws can only be recognized if one has a good knowledge of the original. The same thing holds true in the spiritual realm. The first order of business is to know the original, the written Word of God. It is the believer's obligation to study the Word and know God's program and God's way of doing things today. Then one will be able to recognize the counterfeit because of one's knowledge of the original. Satan's counterfeit program looks very much like the real program of God contained in the pages of Scripture. It will not have obvious flaws.

Therefore, believers must be trained in the Scriptures so they are able to discern the difference between the real and the counterfeit.

The nature of Satan's counterfeit program is found in II Corinthians 11:3-4:

³But I fear, lest by any means, as the serpent beguiled Eve in his craftiness, your minds should be corrupted from the simplicity and the purity that is toward Messiah. ⁴For if he that comes preaches another Yeshua, whom we did not preach, or if ye receive a different spirit, which ye did not receive, or a different gospel, which ye did not accept, ye do well to bear with him.

In verse 4, Paul labeled three things with the word "another": another Yeshua, another spirit, and another gospel. The Greek language has two words that may be translated as "another," but they carry a slightly different meaning. The first term is *allos* and means "another of the same kind." The second term is *heteros*, which means "another of a different kind." With that in mind, a literal rendering of verse 4 would read as follows: "For if he that comes preaches *allon Jesoun*, another Yeshua of the same kind whom we did not preach, or if you receive *pneuma heteron*, another spirit of a different kind, which you have not received, or *euanggelion heteron*, another gospel of a different kind, which you did not accept, you do well to avoid him." The gospel being propagated is declared to be another gospel of a *different* kind. The source is another spirit of a *different* kind. But the Yeshua being presented is another Yeshua of the *same* kind, one who seems like the Messiah of the New Testament but who is a counterfeit.

In II Corinthians 11:13-14, Paul declared:

¹³For such men are false apostles, deceitful workers, fashioning themselves into apostles of Messiah. ¹⁴And no marvel; for even Satan fashions himself into an angel of light.

Those who are propagating a counterfeit Yeshua are declared to be false apostles, but they do not appear as such because they "fashion themselves" to seem like and sound like real ministers of the Messiah. By so doing, they are reflecting their true lord—Satan, the angel of darkness, who fashions himself to appear as an angel of light. The nature of the counterfeit program is to propagate a Yeshua that is very similar to the Messiah of the New Testament, but who is a counterfeit.

The extent of the counterfeit program is expressed by Yeshua in Matthew 7:22-23:

> [22]Many will say to me in that day, Lord, Lord, did we not prophesy by your name, and by your name cast out demons, and by your name do many mighty works? [23]And then will I profess unto them, I never knew you: depart from me, ye that work iniquity.

It should be carefully noted what impostors are able to accomplish in the name of the counterfeit Yeshua. They can cast out demons; they are able to prophesy events which do come to pass; and they perform miracles, such as miracles of healings. Yet, Yeshua will say to them: "I never knew you." Outward manifestations in and of themselves prove nothing, because Satan can duplicate all of them. The real test is never the existence of outward manifestations. The real test is always conformity to Scripture. Is that which is being said, being done, and being taught in conformity with the teachings of the written Word of God? There is no other test by which to judge. In this modern day, when there is so much emphasis on the sensational, on the experiential, and on feelings, many believers are caught up into various "super-spiritual" movements for no other reason than the existence of outward manifestations. By so doing, they never mature in the faith and produce in themselves the kind of fruit that God intends for believers to produce.

To summarize the characteristics of Satan's third abode: Today he dwells in the atmosphere; he has access to heaven as the accuser; he has access to the earth either as a roaring lion for the purpose of destruction or as an angel of light for the purpose of deception. The counterfeit program is spread by counterfeit ministers of Yeshua (II Cor. 11:13) preaching a counterfeit Messiah (II Cor. 11:3) and performing counterfeit signs, miracles, and wonders (Mt. 7:22-23). Another aspect of Satan's third abode is his work of temptation. By causing man to fall, he was able to usurp authority over the earth. To this day, he is still exercising his authority as the prince (Jn. 12:31) and god (II Cor. 4:4) of this world. By causing man to fall, Satan succeeded in keeping man from exercising the authority God

Satanology

had given him over the earth at his creation. The last three abodes of Satan are all future.

D. The Fourth Abode: The Earth

Satan's fourth abode is described in Revelation 12:7-12:

> [7]And there was war in heaven: Michael and his angels going forth to war with the dragon; and the dragon warred and his angels; [8]and they prevailed not, neither was their place found any more in heaven. [9]And the great dragon was cast down, the old serpent, he that is called the Devil and Satan, the deceiver of the whole world; he was cast down to the earth, and his angels were cast down with him. [10]And I heard a great voice in heaven, saying, Now is come the salvation, and the power, and the kingdom of our God, and the authority of his Messiah: for the accuser of our brethren is cast down, who accuses them before our God day and night. [11]And they overcame him because of the blood of the Lamb, and because of the word of their testimony; and they loved not their life even unto death. [12]Therefore rejoice, O heavens, and ye that dwell in them. Woe for the earth and for the sea: because the devil is gone down unto you, having great wrath, knowing that he has but a short time.

In the middle of the tribulation, Satan will be cast out of his present third abode into his fourth abode. He will be confined to the earth for the remainder of the tribulation, for a total of 3½ years. During this time, he will devote all of his attention to destroy the Jewish people once and for all (Rev. 12:6, 13-17). He will attempt to annihilate them by means of the two beasts of Revelation 13 (the Antichrist and the false prophet).

E. The Fifth Abode: The Abyss

Satan's fifth abode is given in Revelation 20:1-3:

> [1]And I saw an angel coming down out of heaven, having the key of the abyss and a great chain in his hand. [2]And he laid hold on the dragon, the old serpent, which is the Devil and Satan, and bound him

81

for a thousand years, ³and cast him into the abyss, and shut it, and sealed it over him, that he should deceive the nations no more, until the thousand years should be finished: after this he must be loosed for a little time.

Satan will be confined in the abyss during the one thousand years of the Messianic kingdom. As a result, sin and death will be greatly reduced on the earth, but not eliminated. During the kingdom, man will exercise authority over the earth. As a result of Satan's confinement in his fifth abode and through the reign of the God-Man, Yeshua the Messiah, man will finally fulfill his calling, as can be seen in Hebrews 2:5-9:

⁵For not unto angels did he subject the world to come, whereof we speak. ⁶But one has somewhere testified, saying, What is man, that you are mindful of him? Or the son of man, that you visit him? ⁷You made him a little lower than the angels; You crowned him with glory and honor, And set him over the works of your hands: ⁸You put all things in subjection under his feet. For in that he subjected all things unto him, he left nothing that is not subject to him. But now we see not yet all things subjected to him. ⁹But we behold him who has been made a little lower than the angels, even Yeshua, because of the suffering of death crowned with glory and honor, that by the grace of God he should taste of death for every man.

F. The Sixth Abode: The Lake of Fire

Satan's sixth abode is described in Revelation 20:7-10:

⁷And when the thousand years are finished, Satan shall be loosed out of his prison, ⁸and shall come forth to deceive the nations which are in the four corners of the earth, Gog and Magog, to gather them together to the war: the number of whom is as the sand of the sea. ⁹And they went up over the breadth of the earth, and compassed the camp of the saints about, and the beloved city: and fire came down out of heaven, and devoured them. ¹⁰And the devil that deceived them was cast into the lake of fire and brimstone, where are also the beast and the false prophet; and they shall be tormented day and night for ever and ever.

The lake of fire will serve as Satan's sixth and final abode, where he will remain for all eternity along with all other fallen angels and unredeemed humanity. As a result of Satan's being cast into his sixth abode, two major effects of his fall will be removed: death (I Cor. 15:24-26) and the seas (Rev. 21:1).

G. Questions and Study Suggestions

Question 1: Where is Satan abiding right now?

Question 2: According to the Scriptures, unbelievers are by default Satan's children. Find the verses that confirm this statement. How does this truth affect your willingness to witness to others?

Study Suggestion 1: Read what John 8:44 says about Satan. Now reflect on what this means for his current abode.

Study Suggestion 2: Matthew 4:9 tells us that Satan desires worship. How does he satisfy this desire in his current abode?

Chapter V

The Works and Judgments of Satan

A. The Work of Satan

Because the Bible has revealed so much about the work of Satan, this section will be divided into nine parts: his work in the cosmos, in the Hebrew Scriptures, in relation to God, in the life of the Messiah, in relation to Gentile nations, in relation to Israel, in relation to unbelievers, in relation to believers, and in the future.

1. In the Cosmos

To understand exactly what "cosmos" means in Scripture, three key Greek words need to be distinguished. The first word is *kósmos*, which means "the world system." It is used 187 times in the New Testament. The second word is *aión*, which is used a total of 41 times. It is usually translated as "world," but a more literal rendering is "age." The term does not refer to how old a person is, but refers to age in the sense of "a period of time." Both *kósmos* and *aión* are frequently translated by the English term "world." The third Greek word is *oikoumené*, also translated as "world." It is used 14 times in the Greek New Testament, but this particular word means "the inhabited world." It does not refer to the world in general, but only to those parts of the world that are inhabited by man.

The one Greek word that concerns Satan is *kósmos*, the world system that is under his control. Of all New Testament authors, the Apostle John was most concerned with this term. Out of the 187 times that *kósmos* is used throughout the New Testament, John alone used it 105 times: 78

times in his Gospel, 23 times in I John, once in II John, and three times in the book of Revelation.

From the 187 usages of the Greek word *kósmos*, a definition and description can be determined. The *kósmos* is an orderly, not a chaotic world. By way of meaning, then, it is the orderly system that is headed up by Satan. Furthermore, the word *kósmos* always has a moral value because it is anti-God in character. It has the concept of worldliness, for it leaves God out. Believers living in the world, in the *kósmos*, come in constant contact with the *kósmos* system.

A more comprehensive definition of the *kósmos* that considers the usages of the Greek word throughout the New Testament would be:

The *kósmos* is a vast order or system that Satan has promoted. It conforms to his ideals, aims, and methods and includes government, conflict, armaments, jealousies, education, culture, religions of morality, and pride.

According to II Peter 3:5-7, this is the world that now exists. It is what Satan employs, and it is a major area where Satan works.

The doctrine of the *kósmos* teaches nine principles. The first principle is that the *kósmos* is under Satan's control. He has authority over the kingdoms of this world (Lk. 4:5-7). He is the prince of this world (Jn. 12:31; 14:30; 16:11) and the god of this age (II Cor. 4:4). John described Satan as being in the world (I Jn. 4:4) and said: *We know that we are of God, and the whole world lies in the evil one* (I Jn. 5:19). More literally, the *kósmos* "lies in the lap" of the evil one. So, the *kósmos* is under Satan's control.

The second principle is that the *kósmos* is absolutely evil. In Romans 5:12, Paul said that sin entered into the *kósmos*, and according to I Corinthians 1:21, the *kósmos* does not know God. The *kósmos* also does not know the Messiah (I Cor. 2:8). Paul speaks of the fornicators of this *kósmos* in I Corinthians 5:10. The *kósmos* is at enmity with God (Jas. 4:4). Peter speaks of the corruption that is in the *kósmos* (II Pet. 1:4) and of the defilement of this world (II Pet. 2:10). This world, this *kósmos*, has the spirit of the antichrist (I Jn. 4:3). Thus, the *kósmos* is wholly evil.

The third principle concerns Satan's undertaking in the *kósmos*, which is temptation in three areas: the lust of the flesh, the lust of the eyes, and the pride of life (I Jn. 2:16).

The fourth principle concerns the three desires of the *kósmos*: First, the world lusts for wealth (Mk. 4:19); second, the world desires security (I Cor. 7:29-31), but apart from God; and third, the world desires material goods (Jas. 2:5), not spiritual things.

The fifth principle concerns the impotence of the *kósmos* as far as spiritual things are concerned. The world does not know the Father (Jn. 17:25); the *kósmos* is without God (Eph. 2:12); and the world does not hear God either (I Jn. 4:5-6).

The sixth principle is that God nevertheless has a love for the *kósmos*: *For God so loved the world, that he gave his only begotten Son* (Jn. 3:16). Because God loved the world, He sent His Son into the *kósmos* (I Jn. 4:9).

The seventh principle is that the Son's program was not of the *kósmos*. He was sent into the world, but He was not of it. He came to rescue believers out of the *kósmos* (Jn. 12:46). The Holy Spirit will convict the *kósmos* (Jn. 16:8). The Messianic kingdom will not be of this *kósmos* (Jn. 18:36).

The eighth principle concerns the believers' position in the *kósmos*. They are not of the *kósmos*. Rather, they are going to be hated by the *kósmos* (Jn. 15:18-19). Believers will have tribulation in the *kósmos* (Jn. 16:33) because they are not of the world (Jn. 17:14, 16), although John 17:18 states that they are sent into the *kósmos*. While believers are in the *kósmos*, they are to be unspotted by it (Jas. 1:27). They will be hated by the *kósmos* (I Jn. 3:13), yet they can overcome it by faith (I Jn. 5:4).

The ninth principle concerns the temporary nature of the *kósmos*. It is destined to come to an end. It is under the judgment of God (Rom. 3:19) and will pass away (I Cor. 7:31). The world is under condemnation (I Cor. 11:32), and there will be the burning of the *kósmos* someday (II Pet. 3:10). The *kósmos* will pass away with the lust thereof (I Jn. 2:17).

2. In the Hebrew Scriptures

Eight specific things can be mentioned concerning Satan's work as related in the Hebrew Scriptures:

1. It was Satan who originated sin in that he was the first sinner.

2. It was Satan who caused the fall of man. Genesis 3:1-8 gives the details of Satan's temptation of Eve, her response, and afterwards, Adam's response. In John 8:44, Satan is called *a murderer* or more literally "a man-slayer," since it is because of his temptations of Adam and Eve that physical death became part of the human experience. In II Corinthians 11:3, Paul stated that Satan *beguiled Eve*. He repeated this statement in I Timothy 2:14.

3. Satan accused Job of having the wrong motives in his love for God (Job 1:6-12; 2:1-6).

4. Satan afflicted Job's possessions and family (Job 1:13-19) and also afflicted Job physically (Job 2:7-8).

5. At Moses' death, Satan disputed with Michael the archangel over the body of Moses (Jude 9). Jude did not state precisely why Satan wanted the body of Moses, but knowing Israel's tendency to commit idolatry, he may have desired to let everyone know where Moses was buried so it would become a center of worship. However, Satan lost that dispute.

6. Satan *moved David to number Israel*, which went contrary to God's law (I Chron. 21:1). As a result, judgment came upon the nation.

7. Satan was the accuser of Israel in the Hebrew Scriptures (Zech. 3:1-2). Today, he accuses the saints.

8. According to Psalm 109:6, Satan was present at the judgment of an unbeliever.

3. In Relation to God

The work of Satan in relation to God is seen in his opposition to God's person. Satan attacked God's veracity and motives by lying about them to Eve in Genesis 3:1-5. According to I John 3:10-12, he opposed the *righteousness* of God.

Another aspect of Satan's work in relation to God is seen in his opposition to God's program. As was seen in the previous chapter of this book, Satan set up a counterfeit program. His fifth "I will" statement ("I will make myself like the Most High") shows that he is the master counterfeiter. He knew he could not be the Most High, so he simply declared his desire to become just *like* the Most High. In order to do this, he instituted his own counterfeit program, which has five facets. The first facet is a counterfeit religion, seen in the following verses:

✧ II Corinthians 11:13-15: *For such men are false apostles, deceitful workers, fashioning themselves into apostles of Messiah. And no marvel; for even Satan fashions himself into an angel of light. It is no great thing therefore if his ministers also fashion themselves as ministers of righteousness; whose end shall be according to their works.*

✧ Revelation 2:9: *I know your tribulation, and your poverty (but you are rich), and the blasphemy of them that say they are Jews, and they are not, but are a synagogue of Satan.*

✧ Revelation 2:13: *I know where you dwell, even where Satan's throne is; and you hold fast my name, and did not deny my faith, even in the days of Antipas my witness, my faithful one, who was killed among you, where Satan dwells.*

This counterfeit religion is not necessarily an obviously false religion. Frequently, it resembles the faith of the New Testament.

The second facet of Satan's counterfeit program is the appearance of counterfeit messiahs, whom he produces in two ways. The first way is by preaching "another Jesus of the same kind." Paul spoke about this satanic ruse in II Corinthians 11:4, when he wrote: *For if he that comes preaches another Yeshua, whom we did not preach, or if ye receive a different spirit, which ye did not receive, or a different gospel, which ye did not accept, ye do well to bear with him.* The Greek word Paul used for "another" is *allon*. It means "another of the same kind."[11] Hence, this counterfeit Yeshua is very similar to the One of the New Testament. The second way Satan

---

[11] This point was discussed extensively in the previous chapter.

produces counterfeit messiahs is by one day raising the Antichrist. This fact is brought out in I John 2:18, 22, and 4:3:

> [2:18]Little children, it is the last hour: and as ye heard that antichrist comes, even now have there arisen many antichrists; whereby we know that it is the last hour . . . [22]Who is the liar but he that denies that Yeshua is the Messiah? This is the antichrist, even he that denies the Father and the Son . . . [4:3]and every spirit that confesses not Yeshua is not of God: and this is the spirit of the antichrist, whereof ye have heard that it comes; and now it is in the world already.

The third facet of Satan's counterfeit program is that he has counterfeit followers. This is seen in Matthew 13:38-39:

> [38]and the field is the world; and the good seed, these are the sons of the kingdom; and the tares are the sons of the evil one; [39]and the enemy that sowed them is the devil: and the harvest is the end of the world; and the reapers are angels.

Satan's counterfeit followers are like tares, a plant that looks very similar to wheat so that it is difficult to tell them apart. By the same token, these counterfeit followers are not the obvious Satan worshippers, but people who actually and publicly affirm their faith in the Messiah, although there are subtle denials.

The fourth facet of Satan's counterfeit program is that he has a counterfeit systematic theology. This fact can be seen in I Timothy 4:1-3:

> [1]But the Spirit says expressly, that in later times some shall fall away from the faith, giving heed to seducing spirits and doctrines of demons, [2]through the hypocrisy of men that speak lies, branded in their own conscience as with a hot iron; [3]forbidding to marry, and commanding to abstain from meats, which God created to be received with thanksgiving by them that believe and know the truth.

Another verse that makes the same point is Revelation 2:24: But to you I say, to the rest that are in Thyatira, as many as have not this teaching, who know not the deep things of Satan, as they are wont to say; I cast upon you none other burden.

The fifth facet of Satan's counterfeit program is that he has the ability to perform counterfeit miracles, a fact that is brought out in Matthew 7:22-23:

> ^{22}Many will say to me in that day, Lord, Lord, did we not prophesy by your name, and by your name cast out demons, and by your name do many mighty works? ^{23}And then will I profess unto them, I never knew you: depart from me, ye that work iniquity.

Another passage that makes the same point is II Thessalonians 2:8-11:

> ^{8}And then shall be revealed the lawless one, whom the Lord Yeshua shall slay with the breath of his mouth, and bring to nought by the manifestation of his coming; ^{9}even he, whose coming is according to the working of Satan with all power and signs and lying wonders, ^{10}and with all deceit of unrighteousness for them that perish; because they received not the love of the truth, that they might be saved. ^{11}And for this cause God sends them a working of error, that they should believe a lie.

These miracles are real miracles, but they are counterfeit in the sense that someone claims to do them in the name of Yeshua, but Messiah is not in them.

4. In the Life of the Messiah

Satan's work is clearly seen in the life of the Messiah. The very first Messianic prophecy, which is in Genesis 3:15, predicted the conflict between Yeshua and Satan. In this verse, God declared: *I will put enmity between you and the woman, and between your seed and her seed: he shall bruise your head, and you shall bruise his heel.* Once Yeshua was born, the conflict began in earnest. Satan tried to kill the Messiah as a babe in Bethlehem. The details are found in Matthew 2:1-18, which records how Herod the Great tried to kill the child. Revelation 12:4 points out that this persecution was inspired by Satan.

Another work of Satan in the life of Yeshua was His temptation (Mt. 4:1-11; Mk. 1:12-13; Lk. 4:1-13). The devil tempted the Messiah to get Him to commit an act of sin.

Satan often used people to try to thwart the work of Messiah and to try to keep Him from His Messianic goal of dying on the cross. For example, he used Herod in Matthew 2:16, Peter in Matthew 16:23, and the multitude in John 8:44 and 59.

Satan also moved Peter to deny Yeshua three times in Luke 22:31, and he was partially responsible for the betrayal of Yeshua by Judas. It was Satan who suggested this betrayal, according to John 13:2. Later, he entered into Judas, in John 13:27. Judas was not merely controlled by a demon; he was controlled by Satan. This is why he was called *the son of perdition* in John 17:12, and as Satan entered Judas, the betrayal was assured.

5. In Relation to the Gentile Nations

Six things can be mentioned regarding the work of Satan among the Gentile nations:

1. It is Satan who lays low the nations (Isa. 14:12). Sometimes nations fall from great heights to become third-, fourth-, or fifth-rate powers because of the work of Satan, who controls the kingdoms of this world.

2. Satan deceives the nations (Rev. 12:9; 20:3).

3. Satan has influence over human governments among the Gentile nations (Dan. 10:13, 20; Mt. 4:8-9; Eph. 6:12).

4. Satan will give his authority over the kingdoms of the world to the Antichrist. At one time, he offered this authority to Yeshua, who rejected it. Satan will make the offer again (Rev. 13:2, 4), this time to the Antichrist, who will accept it.

5. Satan will gather the armies of the nations for the Campaign of Armageddon (Rev. 16:12-16).

6. After Satan is released from his fifth abode, the abyss, he will deceive the Gentiles in the Messianic kingdom and will lead them in one final revolt (Rev. 20:7-10).

6. In Relation to Israel

Simply put, Satan's work in relation to Israel is that he is Israel's adversary. This is found in I Chronicles 21:1 and Zechariah 3:1-2.

7. In Relation to Unbelievers

Eight specific works of Satan among unbelievers can be listed. First, Satan tries to prevent unbelievers from accepting and believing the gospel. Wherever the gospel is proclaimed, he and his agents try to snatch the seed sown in the hearer. This is seen in Matthew 13:19; Mark 4:15; and Luke 8:13. Satan also tries to prevent acceptance of the gospel by blinding the mind of the unbeliever, so that when the gospel is presented, the unbeliever does not comprehend exactly what the issues are. This is seen in II Corinthians 4:3-4.

Second, Satan promotes attraction to falsehood among unbelievers. He does so by indoctrinating people into false religious systems and teaching them false doctrines that satisfy their unregenerate minds (I Tim. 4:1-3; I Jn. 4:1-4). He also promotes attraction to falsehood by teaching a false lifestyle (Eph. 2:1-3; I Jn. 2:15-17).

Third, Satan had the power of death both in relation to believers and unbelievers throughout the history of the Hebrew Scriptures. Hebrews 2:14 and Revelation 1:18 teach that when Yeshua died and entered into the realm of death, He then passed *through* death and took away the keys of death from Satan insofar as believers are concerned. Satan no longer has the authority of death over believers, except in the case of an excommunicated believer, which will be discussed later. However, he still has the authority of death over unbelievers.

Fourth, although Satan causes suffering and oppression among unbelievers in Luke 13:16 and Acts 10:38, not all suffering and oppression is caused by him.

Fifth, Satan sows unbelievers among believers. This is seen in Matthew 13:24-30. These unbelievers are as similar to believers as tare is to wheat. While outwardly they may appear to be saved, there is something wrong and they are not saved.

Sixth, Satan uses unbelievers to pervert the gospel (Acts 13:8-10).

Seventh, Satan has his own ministers whom he produces, fills, and controls. According to II Corinthians 11:13-15, these ministers of Satan are not the obvious type, such as those who head up the churches of Satan. Rather, they *fashion themselves* to sound like and seem like real ministers of the Messiah in order to carry out Satan's work of deception.

Eighth, according to Revelation 2:9-10 and 13, Satan uses unbelievers to oppose the gospel in various ways, either actively or passively.

8. In Relation to Believers

Satan works actively among believers. Twenty points can be made. First, Satan sifts believers the way he sifted Peter in Luke 22:31. The result of this sifting was Peter's denial of Yeshua.

Second, according to I Thessalonians 2:18, Satan hinders believers from accomplishing their calling.

Third, in II Corinthians 2:11, Satan gained advantage over some believers who allowed themselves to be deceived.

Fourth, in II Corinthians 11:3, Satan beguiles some believers, just as he did Eve.

Fifth, according to II Corinthians 12:7, Satan buffets believers, just as he did in the case of Paul.

Sixth, Satan applies physical death to excommunicated believers (I Cor. 5:1-5). As mentioned in point 7, through His death and resurrection, Messiah took the keys of death away from Satan as far as believers are concerned. Ever since, Satan has the power over the death of unbelievers, but he has lost his power over the death of believers, except in the case of a believer who has undergone the four steps of church discipline stated in Matthew 18:15-20. The final step is excommunication, meaning that the believer is put outside the authority of his local church and members of the congregation are admonished not to fellowship with him anymore. He is no longer under the protection of the prayers of the saints of the local church. Furthermore, according to I Corinthians 5:5, he is placed back into Satan's domain for the *destruction of the flesh*. This verse teaches that excommunication will not affect the believer's salvation; he will still be saved, but he will have an untimely death and will not fulfill the calling of God in his life. This is also the *sin unto death* mentioned in I John 5:16.

Seventh, Satan controls some believers from within. It is important to note that the Greek New Testament does not use the term "possession" to describe this control. Rather, it uses the word *pléroó*, which means "to be controlled from within" or "to be demonized." Thus, believers can be controlled from within. An example of this is found in Acts 5:3, where Satan filled Ananias and Sapphira. Peter used the very same words that Paul used in Ephesians 5:18, when he admonished the believers to *be filled with the Spirit*. So, to be filled is "to be controlled from within," and Satan was controlling Ananias and Sapphira from within. In Ephesians 4:27, Paul admonished believers not *to give place to the devil*. The Greek word for "place," *topon*, is a military term that can mean "beachhead." When an army attacks enemy territory, it first tries to establish a beachhead or an area of control within enemy territory. Once this place of control has been established, the army can give covering fire for reinforcements. Giving a beachhead to the devil allows the devil to control that believer from within. This is also confirmed by II Timothy 2:26.

Eighth, according to Ephesians 6:10-18, Satan wars against the saints. This is the reason believers need to wear the whole armor of God.

Ninth, Satan accuses and slanders believers before the throne of God (Rev. 12:10).

Tenth, Satan plants doubts in believers' minds about the truth of God as he did in Eve's mind in Genesis 3:1-5.

Eleventh, Satan incites persecution against believers (Rev. 2:10).

Twelfth, Satan infiltrates the church with false disciples, such as the *tares* of Matthew 13:38-39. He also infiltrates the church with false teachers who preach another Yeshua of the same kind. This is found in II Corinthians 11:13-15 and II Peter 2:1-19.

Thirteenth, Satan promotes division in the churches, causing many congregations to split. This is seen in II Corinthians 2:1-11.

Fourteenth, a major work of Satan among believers is that he tempts them. This is found in I Thessalonians 3:5. Satan tempts believers to lie (Acts 5:3). He tempts them to commit sexual sins (I Cor. 7:5; I Tim. 5:11-15). Paul forbids a husband and wife to refrain too long from sexual intercourse (I Cor. 7:3-5) lest Satan tempt them in that area. Satan also tempts believers to commit specific acts of sin (I Pet. 5:8). He tempts them to be preoccupied with the things of the world (I Jn. 2:15-17; 5:19). Furthermore, Satan tempts believers to develop pride in spiritual matters (I Tim. 3:6). If they do give in to the temptation, they fall into the same sin that brought about Satan's fall. Finally, Satan tempts believers to rely on human wisdom and strength rather than on divine wisdom (I Chron. 21:1-8).

Fifteenth, Satan devours believers (I Pet. 5:8). He draws them so deeply into sin that sometimes they never get out.

Sixteenth, Satan deceives some believers by preaching a counterfeit Yeshua (II Cor. 11:3-4) and by appearing as an angel of light (II Cor. 11:14).

Seventeenth, Satan is responsible for shipwrecking the faith of some believers so that they totally lose their faith. This is seen in I Timothy 1:19-20. Fortunately, even then, they do not lose their salvation.

Eighteenth, Satan employs his demons to try to defeat the saints (Eph. 6:10-12).

Nineteenth, Satan misuses Scripture. This is what he tried to do with Yeshua in Matthew 4:5-6 and Luke 4:9-11. Satan can and does quote Scripture accurately, but he misuses it in that he either quotes it out of context or he gives a misapplication.

Twentieth, Satan uses specific procedures against believers. According to II Corinthians 2:11, he uses *devices* and special designs to entrap the believer. According to Ephesians 6:11, he uses *wiles*. According to I Timothy 3:7 and II Timothy 2:26, he sets out *snares*. Finally, Satan has the power of miracles such as *lying wonders* (II Thess. 2:9). He uses this power for the purpose of working against the saints.

9. In the Future

Five things can be mentioned about Satan's work in the future:
1. He will war against Israel (Rev. 12:13-17).
2. He will energize the Antichrist so that he comes to power (II Thess. 2:9; Rev 13:1-10).
3. He will give rise to the false prophet (Rev. 13:11-18).

4. He will gather the nations for the Campaign of Armageddon (Rev. 16:12-16).

5. He will deceive the nations after the millennium for one last revolt against God's authority (Rev. 20:7-9).

B. The Judgments of Satan

Satan undergoes seven specific judgments. The first three judgments are past history. They occurred at his fall, in Eden, and at the cross of the Messiah. But there are four more judgments yet to come, and they will take place in the middle of the tribulation, at the end of the tribulation, at the Great White Throne, and in the lake of fire.

The first judgment of Satan occurred in Ezekiel 28:16, when he first sinned. The result of the judgment was twofold. First, Satan lost his dual position as *the anointed cherub that covers*, meaning as the canopy over the throne of God, and as the guardian of God's throne. Second, he lost his authority over his first abode, the throne of God, and he lost his authority over his second abode, the mineral garden of Eden.

Satan's second judgment came in Eden as a result of his temptation of Adam and Eve. This judgment is found in Genesis 3:15, where God said to Satan: *I will put enmity between you and the woman, and between your seed and her seed: he shall bruise your head, and you shall bruise his heel.* The judgment was that the woman, whom Satan had tempted, would produce a seed. In the course of many centuries, this descendant of Eve's was going to defeat Satan and would bring life, restoration, and salvation to humanity. A day is coming when this Seed will crush Satan's head.

The third judgment of Satan was at the cross. Satan suffered a specific judgment when the Messiah died. Because Satan knew what was coming, he tried to do everything he could to keep the Messiah from the cross. He constantly tried to have Yeshua killed either prematurely or in the wrong manner, such as by sword or by stoning (Jn. 8:59). But all such attempts failed because Messiah's *hour was not yet come* (Jn. 7:30; 8:20). When Yeshua was finally dying on the cross, Satan was not in control. Rather, the Messiah was totally in control. The cross that brought salvation to humanity brought judgment upon Satan. Yeshua predicted that this would happen in Luke 10:18, when He said, *I beheld Satan fallen as lightning from heaven.* Yeshua stated in John 12:31 that by the virtue of His work, the prince of this world would *be cast out.* Later, He said in John 16:11: *The prince of this world has been judged.* Looking back to the experience of the cross, Colossians 2:14-15 notes that the Messiah *despoiled the principalities and the powers,* one of whom was Satan. By means of His own death and resurrection, Yeshua rendered the devil's power over the death of the believer inoperative (Heb. 2:14-15). By His death, He also destroyed the works of the devil (I Jn. 3:8).

The fourth judgment of Satan will take place in the middle of the tribulation. Satan will be cast out of his present, third abode, the atmospheric heavens, and will be cast into his fourth abode, the earth. He will be confined to the earth for the second half of the tribulation (Rev. 12:7-9). As a result, he will no longer have any access into heaven (Rev. 12:10-12a).

The fifth judgment of Satan will be imprisonment in the abyss during the millennial kingdom (Rev. 20:1-3). As was pointed out, this will be his fifth abode.

The sixth judgment will occur at the Great White Throne. In Romans 16:20 and I Corinthians 6:2-3, Paul said that the church will judge angels. Because good angels do not sin, they have no need to be judged; but fallen angels will be judged by the church, and Satan will be among them.

The seventh and final judgment of Satan will be in the lake of fire. This fact is seen in Matthew 25:41 and Revelation 20:10. The lake of fire will be Satan's sixth abode.

C. The Believer's Responsibility

In the previous discussion on the work of Satan among believers, it was pointed out that Satan attacks believers in twenty different ways. But believers are not left defenseless. They have five options that will help them stand strong against these attacks.

The believer's first defense is described in Ephesians 6:10-18 and in I John 2:14. It is called "the armor of God." This armor is the Scriptures. The more the Scriptures are studied, memorized, and meditated upon, the stronger believers become in their defense against satanic and demonic attacks. Knowing what Scripture has to say about any specific point helps in the fight against Satan. At His temptation, Yeshua was able to counteract Satan by citing Scripture. That was the armor of God for the Messiah, and it is the armor for believers.

The believer's second defense is that he has the power to resist Satan. Believers are told to do so three times: in James 4:7; in I Peter 5:9; and in Ephesians 6:10-18. Believers are never told to go around rebuking Satan, nor are they told to bind him. They are simply admonished to resist him. The best way to accomplish this is by knowing how to apply the right Scripture in any specific temptation one may be confronted with.

The believer's third defense is to stay alert by recognizing how Satan works and by being ready for him. This method is found in I Peter 5:8.

The fourth defense for believers is not active, but passive. It is the intercession of the Messiah. John 17:15, Romans 8:34, and Hebrews 7:25 all make the point that Yeshua is interceding for believers against the evil one.

The fifth and last defense for believers is stated in three principles that should be kept in mind when dealing with Satan and spiritual warfare. The first principle is that believers should not speak of Satan contemptuously. This principle is found in Jude 8-9. Not even the good archangel Michael would issue a railing accusation against Satan. He simply committed the situation to the Lord. Believers should follow his example. They should not go around rebuking Satan, binding him, or calling his name. The second principle is that believers should always keep in mind that Satan may be permitted to inflict certain physical problems on them to teach them a lesson. For instance, Satan was allowed to afflict Job in Job 1-2 so that he could learn more about the sovereign nature of God. Satan was also allowed to afflict Paul in II Corinthians 12:7-16 so that the apostle could learn humility and know that God's strength could be made even greater through Paul's weakness. The third principle for believers in dealing with Satan is that he is sovereignly restricted. Satan is not omnipotent, and even the power he does have cannot be used without God's permission. God will sovereignly restrain Satan and will never allow him to go too far. This truth is seen in Job 1:12 and 2:6.

D. Questions and Study Suggestions

Fill in the blanks:

1. Three Greek words are translated "world" in the New Testament:

    a. The Greek term *aión* literally means _____ (used 41 times).

    b. The Greek term *oikoumené* literally means _____ (used 14 times).

    c. The Greek term *kósmos* is used 187 times in the New Testament, and the specific place in Scripture where this term is used most frequently is _____.

2. The *kósmos*

    a. Means _____ (in contrast to chaos).

    b. Is headed up and promoted by _____ and leaves _____ out.

    c. Is a vast system which conforms to Satan's_____, _____, and _____, and its emphasis is on _____.

    d. Is _____-God.

    e. Is where _____ live.

    f. Includes _____, _____, armaments, jealousies, _____, _____, _____, _____, and pride.

    g. Is the _____ as it now exists.

3. Complete the nine statements concerning the teaching of the cosmos.

    a. The cosmos is under Satan's _____, and as the prince of this world, he has _____ over all the kingdoms of this world.

    b. The cosmos is wholly and totally _____, and as such, the system itself is not _____.

    c. Satan's work or undertaking in the cosmos _____ in three areas.

    d. Striving, struggling, and the things of the cosmos are related to security and _____.

e. The cosmos is utterly impotent as far as _____ things are concerned.

f. God _____ the cosmos and sent His Son into it.

g. Messiah's program and kingdom is _____ the cosmos but not _____ the cosmos.

h. Like Messiah, believers are not _____ the cosmos, so they are _____ by it.

i. The cosmos will _____, because it is under the _____ of God.

4. Before you were saved, you were part of the cosmos system; therefore, personalize each of the next seven verses:

a. I John 5:19 – As part of the world, I _____.

b. James 4:4 – As a friend of the world, I was _____.

c. I John 2:16 – All my greatest desires were not from _____.

d. Mark 4:19 – Things in my life _____ the Word, and it became _____.

e. Ephesians 2:12 – I was _____ from Messiah. I was _____ from the commonwealth of Israel. I was a _____ to the covenants of promise. I had no _____. I was without _____.

f. I John 4:9 – God sent His Son _____ the world, so that I might _____.

g. John 12:46 – Yeshua gave me the opportunity to not remain _____.

h. Personalize the following verses:

   ➤ John 17:16 – As a believer, I am _____ the world.

   ➤ John 15:18-19; I John 3:13 – The world _____ me.

   ➤ John 17:18 – Yeshua has _____ me _____ the world.

   ➤ John 16:33 – In the world, I have _____.

   ➤ I John 5:4 – Being born of God, I can _____ the world by _____.

i. II Peter 3:10 – If I had *not* become a believer, all I valued would be _____.

5. Personal: Have you ever viewed your own salvation on this cosmos-scale? In light of Questions 3-4, could you have rescued yourself out of Satan's cosmos by your own strength? By sheer will power? By your own good deeds? What are your personal thoughts about the salvation that Messiah has accomplished in your life?

6. According to James 1:27, what is your responsibility as a believer in regard to the cosmos?

Part 3:

Demonology

Chapter VI

The Fallen Angels

The English word "demon" comes from the Greek word *daimōn*. This Greek word is used sixty times in the New Testament, 19 times in the singular (*daimōn*) and 41 times in the plural (*daimonia*). Demons are fallen angels. Demonology, then, is the doctrine of demons or the doctrine of fallen angels.

There are five common misconceptions concerning demons that should be mentioned by way of introduction. The reasons these beliefs are wrong will become evident as this study examines what the Bible says about demons. For now, it is sufficient to note these five wrong views.

The first wrong view is that demons simply do not exist. That is, of course, the view of many naturalists and skeptics of the Bible, as well as most unbelievers.

A second wrong view is that demons are not personalities, but evil emanations. In other words, they are merely powers or forces, not personal beings.

A third wrong view is that demons are responsible for every sin. This view is held even by some believers, and it has given rise to a common expression, "The devil made me do it." Sometimes, of course, the devil may have caused one to fall into sin, but in the majority of cases, it is the individual who is responsible, not the devil.

A fourth wrong view teaches that demons are responsible for every form of physical infirmity. Some physical infirmities are caused by demons, but not all.

A fifth wrong view is that demons are responsible for every form of mental illness. As with physical illnesses, demons may indeed be responsible for some mental afflictions, but certainly not for all.

A. The Existence of Demons

There are three ways to show that the Bible teaches the existence of demons. First, the existence of demons is mentioned by every New Testament writer except the author of the book of Hebrews.

- ✤ Matthew mentioned demons in Matthew 4:24; 8:16, 28, 31, 33; 9:32-34; 11:18; 12:22, 24; 15:22; and 17:18.
- ✤ Mark mentioned demons in Mark 1:32, 34; 3:15, 22; 6:13; 7:26, 30; 9:38; and 16:9.
- ✤ Luke mentioned demons in both of his works. They are found in Luke 4:33; 7:33; 8:2, 27, 35, 36, 38; 9:1, 49; and 11:15. In the book of Acts, Luke mentioned them in 5:16; 8:7; 16:16-18; and 19:12-16.
- ✤ John, who wrote a total of five New Testament books, mentioned demons in three of them: in John 8:48-49, 52 and 10:20-21; in I John 4:1-3; and in Revelation 8:10-11; 9:1-21; 12:7, 9; 16:13-14; and 18:2.
- ✤ Paul, who wrote the majority of the books in the New Testament, mentioned demons in three of them: in I Corinthians 10:20-21; in Ephesians 6:12; and in I Timothy 4:1.
- ✤ James mentioned demons in James 2:19 and 3:15.
- ✤ Peter mentioned demons in II Peter 2:4.
- ✤ Jude mentioned demons in Jude 6.

Only the unknown author of the book of Hebrews did not speak about demons. However, he did mention Satan. If he believed in Satan, he obviously believed in the existence of demons.

Second, the existence of demons is confirmed by the teachings and actions of Yeshua. He taught that demons really do exist in Matthew 7:22; 10:8; 12:27-28; 25:41; Mark 7:29; 16:17; Luke 10:20; 11:18-20; and 13:32. Furthermore, He clearly recognized the existence of demons because He cast them out (Mt. 12:22-29; Mk. 1:39; 5:1-20; Lk. 4:35, 41; 8:29-33; 9:42; 11:14).

Third, the Bible clearly teaches the existence of demons in that the disciples, both within and without the apostolic group, recognized it. Matthew 10:1 is an example of the apostolic group acknowledging the reality of demons. Luke 10:17 shows that the seventy disciples, who were outside the apostolic group, recognized the existence of demons as well. There is no question, then, that the Bible clearly teaches that demons exist.

B. The Names of Demons

Demons are given a number of names both in the Hebrew Scriptures and in the New Testament.

1. In the Hebrew Scriptures

The Hebrew Scriptures use a total of twelve names in reference to demons. First, Psalm 78:49 calls them *angels of evil* because that is what they are. The Hebrew word for "angel," *mal'āk*, means "messenger." Demons are messengers of Satan, who is called "the evil one." Therefore, the fallen angels are rightly called angels of evil.

Second, demons are called *sons of God*. The Hebrew term is *banê 'ĕlōhîm*. By itself, it does not distinguish between good angels and fallen angels. Both groups of angels are called sons of God. In Genesis 6:2 and 4, the term refers to evil angels.

Third, demons are called *šēḏîm (shedim)*, a Hebrew word that means "to rule" or "to be lord." This name is used of demons in Deuteronomy 32:17 and Psalm 106:37. It emphasizes a demon's desire to be lord over or to rule a person, either from the inside by indwelling the person or by controlling him and his activities from the outside.

Fourth, fallen angels are called *śə'îrim (seirim)*. Demons are often described as having animal-like features. The word *śə'îrim* refers to demons who have the form of a goat. This explains why satanic groups often use the head of a goat as their symbol. The name appears in Leviticus 17:7; II Chronicles 11:15; Isaiah 13:21; and 34:14.

Fifth, demons are called *lîlît* (*lilit*), a Hebrew word that appears in Isaiah 34:14 and refers to "night demons" or "demons of the night."

Sixth, in I Samuel, an *evil spirit* would fall upon Saul (I Sam. 16:14-16, 23; 18:10; 19:9). In Hebrew, the name is *rūaḥ rā'āh* (*ruach raah*). It emphasizes what a demon is by nature: an evil spirit being, one that has fallen.

Seventh, I Kings 22:22 mentions a *lying spirit*, or in Hebrew a *rūaḥ šeqer* (*ruach seqer*). This term characterizes demons as liars; they are characterized by falsehood.

Eighth, demons are called *familiar spirits* (Deut. 18:11; Isa. 8:19; 19:3). In Hebrew, this name is *hā'ōḇōṯ* (*haobot*), and it means "necromancer" and "medium." Hence, this name is used of demons who are influencing witches, wizards, spiritists, and mediums. Demons who reveal themselves through such people are called "familiar spirits."

Ninth, Genesis 30:11 refers to certain demons as *gāḏ* (*gad*), which means "fortune." Such demons are also mentioned in Isaiah 65:11.

Tenth, Isaiah 65:11 also contains another name for demons, namely, the name *meni*, which means "fate."

Eleventh, demons are called *ĕlîlim* in Psalm 96:5. This name is often translated into English as "idols," but it actually refers to demons of idolatry. Behind all idolatry is the work of demons.

Twelfth, demons are called *qeteḇ* (*qeteb*) in Psalm 91:6. The Hebrew designation means "destruction." It refers to demons who are specifically involved in the work of destruction.

2. In the New Testament

The primary Greek word for "demon" is either *daimōn* or *daimonion*. The first term appears in Matthew 8:31 in reference to evil spirits, while the parallel passage in Luke 8:27 uses *daimonion*. *Daimonion* is the preferred term for demons in the Septuagint and the New Testament, where it appears 63 times. Having the same root, the sense of these ancient Greek words is that a demon is a supernatural agent of intelligence lower than a god. Of importance here is that demons are intelligent beings.

The Greek root of the two words *daimōn* and *daimonion* appears 79 times in the New Testament. In addition to the terms already mentioned, the root also takes the following forms: *daimoniōdēs, daimonizomai, deisidaimonesteros,* and *deisidaimonia. Daimoniōdēs* means "demonic" and "demon-like." The only time this term appears is in James 3:15. *Daimonizomai* means "to be controlled by a demon from within." This form is used 13 times, and one such case is Matthew 4:24. *Deisidaimonesteros* means "to be very reverent to demons," "to be very fearful of gods," or "to be superstitious." This term emphasizes the occult world. The only time it is used is in Acts 17:22. The last form of the root word for "demon," *deisidaimonia,* means "demon worship," "religion," and "superstition." This term is also strongly connected with the occult world and is used only once, in Acts 25:19.

Besides these Greek words that all come from the same root, there are five Greek terms that are generally translated by the English word "spirit." They are used a total of 46 times in conjunction with demons.

1. The expression *pneuma ponēron* is translated as "evil spirit" in Luke 7:21 and Acts 19:12-13, 15-16.

2. The phrase *pneuma akathartos* means "unclean spirit" and is found in Matthew 10:1; 12:43; Mark 1:27; 3:11; 5:13; Acts 5:16; 8:7; and Revelation 16:13.

3. The expression *pneumata ponērotera* means "more wicked spirits" and is found in Luke 11:26.

4. The phrase *pneuma planos* refers to seducing spirits in I Timothy 4:1.

5. The last Greek phrase combines "spirit" and "demon" as *pneumata daimoniōn,* or *spirits of demons,* in Revelation 16:14.

As was stated in Chapter I of this book, the Greek term for "angel" is *angelos.* It means "messenger." In Matthew 25:41 and Revelation 12:7-9, demons are referred to as angels because they are Satan's messengers.

Finally, there is one special designation for the demon of the abyss. In Hebrew, his name is *Abaddon,* and his Greek name is *Apollyon.* Both names are found in Revelation 9:11. Whether the Hebrew or Greek name is used, the meaning is the same. The demon of the abyss is a demon of destruction.

C. The Personality of Demons

Demons are not mere emanations or forces. They have personality. This can be seen both by the fact that they possess certain attributes of personality and by the personal pronouns used in describing these created beings.

As was seen in the previous chapters on angels and on Satan, there are three attributes of personality: intellect, emotion, and will. If it can be proven that something has all three of these attributes, then that something is a personality.

There are six ways to prove that demons have intellect. First, they know who Yeshua is (Mk. 1:24). Second, they know their own future doom (Mt. 8:28-29). Third, they knew Paul (Acts 16:17-18; 19:15). Fourth, they know *that God is one* (Jas. 2:19). Fifth, they have a counterfeit system of doctrine (I Tim. 4:1-3). And sixth, demons have the ability to communicate by speech (Lk. 4:34-35, 41; 8:28-31). Very clearly, demons do have intellect, the first attribute of personality.

There is also no question that demons have emotion. Matthew 8:28 shows some demons reacting with the emotion of anger to the arrival of the Messiah. The subsequent verse, Matthew 8:29, proves that they have the emotion of fear (see also Jas. 2:19).

Finally, there are three ways to prove that demons have will. First, they have the will to make requests (Mt. 8:31; Lk. 8:32). Second, they have the will to obey commands and orders (Mk. 1:27; Lk. 4:35-36). Third, they have the will to leave a person, seek a new place to live, or return to the place where they formerly lived (Mt. 12:43-45). All of these examples show that demons exercise will. Since demons have intellect, emotion, and will, they have personality.

Regarding personal pronouns, when the New Testament speaks of demons, it uses words such as "we," "us," "they," "your," "I," and "me." Demons are never referred to as "it," which would be the proper grammatical form if demons were mere emanations. Examples of the usage of the above-mentioned pronouns are Mark 5:6-13 and Luke 8:28-30.

The use of personal pronouns, in addition to the attributes of intellect, emotion, and will, clearly show that demons are real personalities.

D. The Origin of Demons

All demons have the same origin. They are the angels who fell with Satan at the time of his fall. All demons were originally free, but some of them have since been confined. It will be necessary to draw that distinction in discussing the origin of demons.

1. The Origin of Free Demons

To understand the origin of free demons, it is necessary to recognize that demons and fallen angels are one and the same rather than two separate categories of beings. That they are the same can be seen in five ways.

First, both demons and fallen angels are said to have a similar relationship to Satan. Satan, who is an angel, is called *the prince of demons* in Matthew 12:24. This title indicates that those who follow him are also angels. Ephesians 6:11-12 points out that Satan has a well-organized order of angels, and it is very reasonable to suppose that these ranks of angels are demons. In Matthew 25:41, they are referred to as the "devil's angels." In all likelihood, they are demons. They are also called "Satan's angels" in Revelation 12:7-9. This, too, points to them as being the same as demons. These four passages show that fallen angels and demons have a similar relationship to Satan, implying that they are one and the same.

Second, fallen angels and demons have the same essence of being; both are spirit beings.

Third, demons and fallen angels conduct similar activities in that both seek to enter people, and both war against man and God. Fallen angels are seen doing this in Revelation 9:1-2, 11, and 13-15; demons are seen doing the same thing in Revelation 9:3-10 and 16-21. This indicates that fallen angels and demons are the same.

Fourth, demons and fallen angels share the same abode. They dwell in the atmospheric heavens (Eph. 2:2; 6:12; Rev. 12:7-12).

Fifth, in all biblical texts, one finds either fallen angels or demons, but never both. Every applicable passage speaks of either one or the other. This, too, shows that they are one and the same creatures.

Once it is understood that fallen angels and demons are one and the same, the origin of free demons can then also be understood. Free demons, who are fallen angels, originated at the time of the fall of Satan in that demons are the angels who fell with him (Rev. 12:4). There were three results of their fall:

1. They lost their original holiness.
2. They became corrupt in nature and conduct, as the various Old and New Testament names for demons demonstrate.
3. They became the demons of Satan.

2. The Origin of Confined Demons

In discussing the origin of confined demons, another distinction must be made because there are two different categories of confined demons: temporarily confined demons and permanently confined demons.

a. Temporarily Confined Demons

Some demons are confined temporarily after being cast out of a person. The demon Legion of Luke 8:30 did not wish to be sent into the place of confinement; instead, he asked to be allowed to go into the pigs. Some demons are confined temporarily after being cast out and then released later.

Many others are confined temporarily now, but are to be released for specific judgments of the tribulation. Revelation 9:1-11 speaks of the release of demons for a period of five months to torment men to a great degree, but short of death. Revelation 9:13-21 speaks of the release of two hundred million demons for the purpose of killing one-third of the world's population.

The place of temporary confinement for theses demons is the abyss. Some are confined there now and will be released during the tribulation, while others are temporarily confined there after being cast out, to be released later to do Satan's bidding again.

b. Permanently Confined Demons

The second category is demons who have been confined permanently and will never be released. These are demons who will move directly into the lake of fire after the Great White Throne Judgment.

There are three key passages that deal with these permanently confined demons: Genesis 6:1-4; II Peter 2:4-5; and Jude 6-7.

(1) Genesis 6:1-4

A major area of debate among believers is whether the first passage, Genesis 6:1-4, refers to angels. The purpose of this segment is to show that it does, in fact, refer to angels who are now permanently confined. In order to prove this case, it will be necessary to study these verses phrase by phrase in some detail.

> ¹And it came to pass, when men began to multiply on the face of the ground, and daughters were born unto them, ²that the sons of God saw the daughters of men that they were fair; and they took them wives of all that they chose. ³And Jehovah said, My Spirit shall not strive with man for ever, for that he also is flesh: yet shall his days be a hundred and twenty years. ⁴The Nephilim were in the earth in those days, and also after that, when the sons of God came in unto the daughters of men, and they bare children to them: the same were the mighty men that were of old, the men of renown.

Verse 1 speaks of the multiplication of humanity before the Flood. The Hebrew word for "men," *hā'āḏām* (*ha-adam*) is generic and refers to humanity in general, including both men and women. As such, the word cannot be limited to the sons of Cain, as some assume. Rather, it includes both Sethites and Cainites, and both of these groups died in the Flood. The Hebrew word for "daughters," *ūḇānōwṯ* (*ubanowt*), means "and females." The emphasis here is on the female portion of humanity. Again, the expression cannot be limited, as some teach, to the female descendants of Cain. The Hebrew term simply refers to the female portion of the population. Combining what has been said so far, verse 1 could read:

113

"Humanity multiplied, and females were born unto them." The distinction in verse 1 is not between male Sethites and female Cainites. Rather, the emphasis is on the female portion of humanity in general, which would include both Cainites and Sethites.

Verse 2 speaks about the intermarriage of these women with the sons of God. There are two key expressions that need to be discussed: "the sons of God" and "the daughters of men."

The Hebrew expression for "sons of God," *banê 'ĕlōhîm*, and the basic meaning of the phrase is "to be brought into existence by God's creative act." This meaning is found in Luke 3:38 in speaking of Adam. It is also the meaning when believers are called "the sons or children of God" in the New Testament. But in the Hebrew Bible, *banê 'ĕlōhîm* always refers to angels, whether holy or fallen. Examples are Job 1:6 and 2:1, where Satan was among the sons of God, and Job 38:7, where the sons of God were present at creation. The Septuagint uses the same term in Deuteronomy 32:8, where it refers to angels.[12] No one debates that the other places where the expression is found in the Hebrew Scriptures clearly refer to angels. But some want to make Genesis 6:1-4 the one exception, even though there is simply no warrant for making such an exception here. In the New Testament, the phrase "sons of God" is expanded. Adam is called "the son of God" in Luke 3:38, because he was brought into existence by creation. Believers are called "sons of God" in John 1:12, because they are considered to be a new creation (Gal. 6:15). But again, in Genesis, the text is dealing with the specific Hebrew expression *banê 'ĕlōhîm*. As the term is used in the Hebrew Scriptures, it is always used of angels. The distinction in Genesis 6:2, then, is not between Sethites and Cainites, but between humanity and angels. The word "men" emphasizes humanity; the phrase "sons of God" emphasizes angels.

The phrase "daughters of men" is a generic term for women. It includes females of both Sethite and Cainite descent. Verse 2 is saying that *the sons of God saw the daughters of men.* Some have interpreted this verse to mean "godly males intermarried with ungodly females." However, the expression "daughters of men" simply means "womankind," and the phrase "sons of God" refers to angels. If the meaning is kept consistent

---

[12] As to the variation of this phrase, see Chapter 1 of this book.

with its usage elsewhere in the Old Testament, the passage is clearly speaking of fallen angels intermarrying with human women.

There are two other points that support this interpretation. First, the intermarriage only goes one way. It is always sons of God marrying daughters of men. There is no record of "daughters of God" marrying "sons of men." If the distinction was between Sethites and Cainites, it simply would not happen this way. In human society, intermarriage occurs both ways. Today, saved men sometimes marry unsaved women, and vice versa. If the other claim were true, it would mean that male Sethites married female Cainites, but that male Cainites never married female Sethites, which would be extremely unlikely. Intermarriage would thus be confined to godly men with ungodly women, but not godly women with ungodly men. But there is only a one-way intermarriage in Genesis 6: the sons of God intermarrying with the daughters of men. Second, the context clearly speaks of a cohabitation that was unusual and unnatural and caused the worldwide Flood. Verses 1-4 deal with the angelic cause of the Flood, while verses 5-6 deal with the human cause. Cohabitation between Sethites and Cainites would not be unusual or unnatural, while cohabitation between angels and humans is both.

Those who do not like this teaching object to it by quoting Yeshua, who said in Matthew 22:30: *For in the resurrection they neither marry, nor are given in marriage, but are as angels in heaven.* The claim is made that this verse teaches that angels are sexless beings. However, the verse states something else. It says that in the resurrection and in heaven, human beings do not marry, nor are they given in marriage. Then the verse mentions the angels in heaven. It is important to note that the comparison is not with angels in general, but with angels in heaven. The emphasis is that in heaven, good angels neither marry nor are they given in marriage. The same is true with human beings. In heaven, they do not marry, nor are they given in marriage. Humans on earth, on the other hand, clearly do marry and are given in marriage. Genesis 6:1-4 is speaking of angels on earth. Another line of evidence is that angels are never declared to be sexless beings. In fact, in both the Hebrew Scriptures and the New Testament, angels are always described in the masculine gender, not in the feminine, nor in the neuter. Whenever angels become visible, they always appear as young men, never as women (Gen. 18:1-19:22; Mk. 16:5-

7; Lk. 24:4-7; Acts 1:10-11). Matthew 22:30 does not teach that angels are sexless beings, nor can the verse be used as an argument against the angelic interpretation of Genesis 6:1-4, because this passage is dealing with a situation on earth, not in heaven.

The reason Satan bothered to have some of his fallen angels intermarry with human women can be understood by investigating the greater context of Genesis. Three chapters earlier, the first Messianic prophecy is recorded: *I will put enmity between you and the woman, and between your seed and her seed: he shall bruise your head, and you shall bruise his heel* (Gen. 3:15). This prophecy declared that the Messiah would be born of the seed of the woman, and this seed would crush the head of Satan. What was happening in Genesis 6:1-4 was a satanic attempt to corrupt the seed of the woman by having some of his angels take on human form (again, angels always appear as young males when they take on human form) and intermarry with human women to try to corrupt the seed. Thus, the events of Genesis 6:1-4 were a satanic attempt to nullify the prophecy of Genesis 3:15.

Genesis 6:3 declares the judgment of God. With the words, *And Jehovah said*, the oracle of judgment is introduced: *My spirit shall not strive with man for ever.* The Hebrew word for "strive" is *yāḏôn* (*yadon*), a word that appears only once in the entire Bible. There are two possible meanings of this term. If *yāḏôn* comes from the Hebrew root *dîn* and means "to strive," then the striving refers to the restraining of sin; the Spirit was striving in the sense of restraining sin through the preaching of Enoch and Noah. However, if the meaning is "to remain," from the Hebrew root *danan*,[13] then it means that the spirit of life, which God breathed into man, will not remain in man. The use of the Hebrew word *lə'ōlām* (*le-olam*) for "forever" means that God will not allow the race to continue forever in such a sin as described in Genesis 6:2. There will be a limit. Then God added: *for that he* [man] *also is flesh.* This is the reason for the restraining. Humans are flesh; they have the sin nature. So, in contrast to the eternal spirit, man is flesh, and he is subject to death. God concludes His judgment by mentioning the allotted time: *Yet shall his days be a*

---

[13] For additional information, see: Richard M. Davidson, "The Nature and Work of the Holy Spirit in the Pentateuch" (2016). *Faculty Publication*. 862. Available on the internet at https://digitalcommons.andres.edu/pubs/862.

hundred and twenty years. These are the years remaining before the Flood, a 120-year period of grace. As I Peter 3:20 puts it: *when the long-suffering of God waited in the days of Noah, while the ark was a preparing*. From the initial decree, God gave to humanity a period of 120 years so that they could repent. This was a measure of His grace.

Genesis 6:4 goes on to describe the results of the intermarriage between fallen angels and human women: *The Nephilim were in the earth in those days*. The word "Nephilim" means "fallen ones." Some Bible translators interpreted the word as "giants": *There were giants in the earth in those days*. However, the reason for choosing the word "giant" is not based upon the Hebrew, but on the Septuagint, which translated the Hebrew word *nafilîm* (*nefilim*) by the Greek word *gigantes*. This Greek term is the source of the English word "giant," but it does not quite mean the same thing. Rather, it corresponds to the Latin *titanas*, the root of the English word "Titans." In Greek mythology, Titans were part man and part god. When the Jewish translators of the Septuagint were trying to find a Greek word that would express to the Greek reader what the Nephilim were, the best word they could come up with was *gigantes*. In English, however, the word "giants" gives the wrong connotation, namely, that of creatures who are huge in size. However, Genesis 6:4 goes on to say: *Also after that, when the sons of God came unto the daughters of men, and they bore children to them: the same were the mighty men that were of old, the men of renown*. The verse explains how the Nephilim came into being. They were the children of human women and fallen angels. They were human on one side, but superhuman on the other. The Hebrew word for "mighty men" is *giborim*. Because of their unique origin, the Nephilim proved to be exceptional, and the intermarriage of fallen angels and human women produced a grotesque race that was superhuman both mentally and physically in strength, but not necessarily in size. Therefore, rather than trying to find a proper translation of the Hebrew word *Nephilim*, it is best to transliterate the term or to speak of "fallen ones."

(2) II Peter 2:4-5

This passage provides information about the location of the permanently confined demons:

> [4] *For if God spared not angels when they sinned, but cast them down to hell, and committed them to pits of darkness, to be reserved unto judgment;* [5] *and spared not the ancient world, but preserved Noah with seven others, a preacher of righteousness, when he brought a flood upon the world of the ungodly;*

The temporarily confined demons are found in the abyss, but the permanently confined demons are elsewhere. The Greek word translated in this passage as "hell" is *Tartarus*. Like the abyss, Tartarus is a section of *Sheol* or Hades where the permanently confined demons are kept. The abyss is for demons who are temporarily confined, but Tartarus is for demons who are permanently confined. Tartarus is referred to as *pits of darkness*, and these angels are reserved there until the Great White Throne Judgment, the final judgment. This means that at no time will these angels ever be released. They will go directly from Tartarus to stand before the Great White Throne Judgment, and then they will be cast into the lake of fire. There will never be a time when they will be free to roam; they are permanently confined.

The timing of their confinement is revealed in verse 5 and was in conjunction with the Flood. This agrees well with the events of Genesis 6:1-4 that are also connected with the Flood. The purpose of the Flood was to destroy the Nephilim, who were a product of fallen angels and human women.

By comparing II Peter 2:4-5 with Genesis 6:1-4, there is good evidence to show that Genesis is not speaking about Sethites intermarrying with Cainites, but fallen angels intermarrying with human women. This is a valid conclusion just from a study of the Hebrew Scriptures themselves. However, the New Testament also supports this particular interpretation.

(3) Jude 6-7

Jude 6-7 emphasizes the fall of a select group of angels:

> [6] *And angels that kept not their own principality, but left their proper habitation, he has kept in everlasting bonds under darkness unto the judgment of the great day.* [7] *Even as Sodom and Gomorrah, and the cities about them, having in like manner with these given themselves*

over to fornication and gone after strange flesh, are set forth as an
example, suffering the punishment of eternal fire.

The fall of these angels is described in four statements. First, they *kept*
not their own principality. The word "principality" is frequently used of
the angelic realm and is one of the various ranks within the angelic realm.
It means that these angels did not remain in their position and place of
rank within the satanic cosmos. Second, they *left their proper habitation*.
They left the demonic-angelic sphere of operation and entered into the
human sphere by taking on the form of young men and intermarrying
with human women. Third, they are now *kept in everlasting bonds under*
darkness. Here, Jude mentioned the same thing as Peter: These angels
are now permanently confined. Fourth, these fallen angels are to be kept
in Tartarus until *the judgment of the great day*. Jude affirms Peter's statements that these angels are being kept in bondage until the Great White
Throne Judgment and will never be free again.

The nature of their sin is dealt with in verse 7. The key phrase is "in like
manner." In like manner as Sodom and Gomorrah, these angels went after strange flesh. The sin committed by these angels is similar to the sexual sin of Sodom and Gomorrah, that of going after strange flesh.
"Strange flesh" means sexual union that is contrary to nature. In the case
of Sodom and Gomorrah, the strange flesh was homosexuality. In the
case of these angels, the strange flesh was female flesh. Instead of remaining in their usual state of residence, these fallen angels invaded a
new state of residence of alien flesh to commit gross sexual immorality.
So, the men of Sodom and Gomorrah and these angels have one thing in
common: They are guilty of sexual sins.

By comparing Genesis 6:1-4 with II Peter 2:4-5 and Jude 6-7, it is clear
that these were angels who intermarried with human women, not simply
Sethites who intermarried with Cainites.

3. Summary

All demons have the same origin in that they fell with Satan. However, at
some point after the fall, some of Satan's angels married human women
for the purpose of trying to corrupt the seed of the woman in order to
thwart the first Messianic prophecy, that of Genesis 3:15. These

particular angels are now permanently confined in Tartarus. The others are free; but periodically, many of them are temporarily confined in the abyss before eventually being released to roam free again. The difference between temporary confinement and permanent confinement con be compared to receiving a jail sentence versus a life sentence. Eventually, of course, all demons will be eternally confined in the lake of fire following the Great White Throne Judgment.

E. The Number of Demons

According to Hebrews 12:22-24, God created innumerable angels. The Scriptures also provide several indications that there are a great number of demons. For example, Mark 5:9, 15, and Luke 8:30 mention a legion of demons residing in one person. A legion of soldiers consists of anywhere from four thousand to six thousand men. So, this one person had between four to six thousand demons residing in him. Revelation 9:16 mentions two hundred million temporarily confined demons.

While the Scriptures never specify an exact number of demons, Revelation 12:3-4 reveals the percentage of angels that fell with Satan:

3And there was seen another sign in heaven: and behold, a great red dragon, having seven heads and ten horns, and upon his heads seven diadems. 4And his tail drew the third part of the stars of heaven, and did cast them to the earth: and the dragon stands before the woman that is about to be delivered, that when she is delivered he may devour her child.

Verse 4 states that the dragon, who is Satan, drew with him one-third of the stars. It was already pointed out in this book that whenever the word "star" is used symbolically, it is always the symbol for an angel. The fact that Satan drew one-third of the stars reveals that out of the entire body of angels, one-third followed him in his original revolt. One-third of the original number of angels became demons, while two-thirds remained loyal to God.

F. The Organization of Demons

The fallen angels are as organized as the good angels. They have the same titles and ranks. For example, I Corinthians 15:24 states: *Then comes the end, when he shall deliver up the kingdom to God, even the Father; when he shall have abolished all rule and all authority and power.* According to this verse, the ranks in the organization of demons are "rule," "authority," and "power."

Ephesians 6:12 lists "powers," "principalities," and "world-rulers," stating: *For our wrestling is not against flesh and blood, but against the principalities, against the powers, against the world-rulers of this darkness, against the spiritual hosts of wickedness in the heavenly places.*

Colossians 2:15 also mentions "principalities" and "powers": *having despoiled the principalities and the powers, he made a show of them openly, triumphing over them in it.*

The Hebrew Scriptures tell of demons who function as rulers over nations, such as *the prince of the kingdom of Persia* in Daniel 10:13 and *the prince of Greece* in Daniel 10:20.

It is obvious that the organization of demons is an imitation of the organization of elect angels, with similar ranks and orders. Since Satan and all demons were once part of the divine order of creation, they were well aware of the hierarchical structure God has set up in heaven.

G. The Characteristics of Demons

The characteristics of demons can be divided into three categories: their nature, their power, and their morality.

1. Their Nature

Four things should be mentioned concerning the nature of demons. First, they are spirit beings. In fact, they are the same as unclean spirits. This is obvious by comparing parallel accounts. For example, Matthew 17:18 mentions a demon, but the parallel account in Mark 9:25 calls him an "unclean spirit." We also find the terms "demon" and "unclean spirit" used interchangeably in Matthew 8:16; Luke 9:38-39, 42; 10:17, and 20. The fact that the Scriptures use these terms correspondently shows that demons are spirit beings. Because of this feature, a great number of them can exist in a small space, as seen in Luke 8:30, where a legion of demons resides in one human body. Furthermore, Ephesians 6:12 confirms that demons are not composed of flesh and blood.

Second, as spirits who are not made of flesh and blood, demons are bodiless. This can be seen in Matthew 12:43-45 and Mark 5:12. They can enter a physical body, but they do not have bodies of their own.

Third, while demons are spirit beings, they have clear shapes and features, which are frequently animal-like. This is seen in Revelation 9:7-10, 17-19; and 16:13-14.

Fourth, demons seek to control human beings, as their power is to some extent dependent upon their inhabitation of man. This is found in Mark 5:1-13; Acts 16:16; and 19:16.

2. Their Power

Regarding the power of demons, Mark 5:1-5 and Acts 19:16 show that demons have the power to control human beings from within. They can also afflict people. This is seen in Revelation 9:1-21, which states that demons will afflict unbelievers in the tribulation for five months. Furthermore, demons can perform miracles (Rev. 16:14). Finally, they have the ability to appear visibly (Rev. 9:7-10, 17-19; 16:13-14).

3. Their Morality

Nine things should be noted concerning the morality of demons:

1. As mentioned above, they are called *unclean spirits* (Mt. 10:1; Mk. 1:23, 27; 3:11; 5:2; 9:25; Lk. 4:36; Acts 8:7; Rev. 16:13). The term "unclean" defines the morality of demons.
2. They are *evil spirits* (Lk. 7:21), corrupt in their nature.
3. They act fiercely and viciously (Mt. 8:28).
4. They are also vile and malicious (Lk. 9:39).
5. They are characterized by extreme viciousness (Mk. 9:20).

6. They have a counterfeit system of doctrine (I Tim. 4:1-3). This counterfeit system has at least six points: apostasy from the faith; giving in to seduction (v. 1a); living a life of hypocrisy (v. 2a); having a lying tongue (v. 2a); loss of the exercise of conscience (v. 2b); and denial of the liberty of the believer in the areas of marriage and eating (v. 3).

7. Their immorality leads to further immorality (Lk. 8:27).

8. They are described as being part of *this darkness* controlled by Satan (Eph. 6:12).

9. There are varying degrees of wickedness even among demons (Mt. 12:43-45).

H. The Activities of Demons

The activities of demons will be discussed in four categories: historical activities, general activities, particular activities, and occult activities.

1. Historical Activities

Demonic activity increases and decreases at certain periods of time. Throughout the Hebrew Scriptures, very little demonic activity was recorded. But with Gospel history, there was a sudden inundation of demonic activity. Suddenly, demons were everywhere and Yeshua was confronted with them wherever He went. The reason for this is found in Revelation 12:1-5:

> *¹And a great sign was seen in heaven: a woman arrayed with the sun, and the moon under her feet, and upon her head a crown of twelve stars; ²and she was with child; and she cries out, travailing in birth, and in pain to be delivered. ³And there was seen another sign in heaven: and behold, a great red dragon, having seven heads and ten horns, and upon his heads seven diadems. ⁴And his tail draws the third part of the stars of heaven, and did cast them to the earth: and the dragon stands before the woman that is about to be delivered, that when she is delivered, he may devour her child. ⁵And she was delivered of a son, a man child, who is to rule all the nations with a*

rod of iron: and her child was caught up unto God, and unto his throne.

Around the time of Yeshua's first coming, Satan brought his demonic cohort from their present abode in the atmospheric heavens down to the earth. They did not come to the earth in general, but specifically to the Middle East and particularly to Israel. Satan brought the majority, perhaps all, of his demons into this area in an attempt to thwart the purpose of the first coming of Yeshua. He manipulated events and people to try to keep the Messiah from the cross by having Him killed either prematurely as a babe in Bethlehem or in a wrong manner, such as by the sword or by stoning. Then, as history moved on to the book of Acts and beyond, demonic activity was reduced to the level that it was in the Hebrew Scriptures. In his Gospel, Luke recorded the presence and activities of demons everywhere. But when he wrote Acts, the longest book in the New Testament, he mentioned demons in only four passages.

In the future, during the tribulation, there will once again be heavy demonic activity. The book of Revelation mentions demons so frequently that it seems demonic activity will approximate the level of what it was in the Gospel stage, and it will be for a similar purpose: to try to thwart the second coming of the Messiah. The second coming will not occur until the Jewish people ask Yeshua to return. Knowing this, Satan will use all of his demons during the tribulation in an attempt to move the entire world against the Jews. If he were to succeed in annihilating the Jewish people once and for all before they can plead for Messiah to come back, Yeshua would not return. Therefore, Satan's hope is to destroy the Jews before the national regeneration of Israel. Then there would be no second coming, and Satan's career would be eternally safe. For that reason, there will be an increase in demonic activity in the tribulation.

In summary, the history of demonic activity can be divided into four eras:

1. There was little activity from Genesis until the Gospels.
2. There was tremendous activity during the history of the Gospels.
3. From Acts until the tribulation, demonic activity is reduced.
4. There will once again be a tremendous increase in demonic activity during the tribulation.

2. General Activities

In a general sense, demons are involved in three main activities. First, they try to thwart the purpose of God. One example of this is found in Daniel 10:10-14, where it is recorded that a leading demon held an angel of God captive for three weeks to try to prevent God's revelation to Daniel of things to come. Another example is described in Revelation 16:12-16, where demons will aid in gathering the nations for the Campaign of Armageddon to try to halt God's plan for the second coming.

A second general activity of demons is to extend Satan's authority over his cosmos by doing his bidding. This is seen in Ephesians 2:1-2:

> *¹And you did he make alive, when ye were dead through your trespasses and sins, ²wherein ye once walked according to the course of this world, according to the prince of the powers of the air, of the spirit that now works in the sons of disobedience;*

This activity is the reason Paul urged believers in Ephesians 6:11-12 to put on the whole armor of God:

> *¹¹Put on the whole armor of God, that ye may be able to stand against the wiles of the devil. ¹²For our wrestling is not against flesh and blood, but against the principalities, against the powers, against the world-rulers of this darkness, against the spiritual hosts of wickedness in the heavenly places.*

A third general activity of demons is to do God's bidding. Demons can be and are used by God to carry out His own purposes, plan, and will. For example, in I Samuel 16:14, a demon was used to torment Saul: *Now the Spirit of Jehovah departed from Saul, and an evil spirit from Jehovah troubled him.* In I Kings 22:19-23, a lying demon was used to arrange for the death of Ahab. In II Corinthians 12:7, a demon was allowed to be used to keep Paul humble: *And by reason of the exceeding greatness of the revelations, that I should not be exalted overmuch, there was given to me a thorn in the flesh, a messenger of Satan to buffet me, that I should not be exalted overmuch.* So, God will use demons to carry out His own purposes.

3. Particular Activities

Demons are not only involved in historical and general activities, but also in twelve specific or particular activities that should be noted:

1. Demons are linked to the control of nations. Daniel 10:10-14 and 10:20-21 show that just as God has good angels controlling nations, Satan has evil angels doing the same.

2. Demons can and do inflict physical maladies. For instance, a demon inflicted dumbness or muteness in Matthew 9:32-33; 12:22; and Mark 9:17. Certain demons inflicted deafness in Mark 9:25. They inflicted curvature of the spine in Luke 13:10-13. They inflicted epilepsy in Matthew 17:15-18; Mark 9:20; and Luke 9:37-42. They inflicted blindness in Matthew 12:22. And they inflicted personal injury in Mark 9:18. Hence, demons can cause physical illnesses. However, it is important to note that there is a difference between physical problems caused by human frailty and those caused by demons (see, for example, Matthew 4:24 and 8:16).

3. Demons cause insanity (Mk. 5:1-5; Lk. 8:26-27).

4. They give great physical strength (Mk. 5:1-4; Lk. 8:29).

5. They cause suicide (Mk. 9:22).

6. Demons possess animals (Mk. 5:12-13).

7. Demons promote idolatry (Lev. 17:7; Deut. 32:17; Isa. 65:11; Zech. 13:2; Hos. 4:12; Acts 17:22-23; I Cor. 10:20).

8. They cause people to worship demons (Rev. 9:20-21).

9. Demons cause impurity and immorality (Lk. 8:27).

10. They promote false doctrine (I Tim. 4:1; Jas. 3:15; I Jn. 4:1).

11. They oppose the spiritual growth of believers (Eph. 6:12).

12. They attempt to separate believers from the love of God (Rom. 8:38).

Demons also control humans from within, but this is something to be studied in a different context.

4. Occult Activities

The activities of demons in relation to the occult world can be divided into five units: Greek words, facets of the occult world, characteristics of occultism, snares and practice of occultism, and the Bible and occultism.

a. The Greek Words

There are three Greek words that connect demonism with the world of the occult. The first word is *deisidaimonia*, which means "a reverence for demonic things." This term is found in Acts 25:19. The second Greek word is *deisidaimonesteros*, which means "a reverence for demons." This term is found in Acts 17:22. The third Greek word is *daimoniōdēs*, which literally means "demonic things," found in James 3:15.

From these Greek words and the verses where they are found, we can derive a basic meaning of the occult. The term "occult" refers to things that are covered over, hidden and concealed, secret, and mysterious. These four elements help to define the meaning of occult, and they show that occult practices are an attempt to go beyond the five senses in order to gain hidden knowledge and understanding.

b. The Facets of the Occult World

Three passages of Scripture need to be considered in dealing with the facets of the occult world. The first passage is Deuteronomy 18:9-14:

> *⁹When you are come into the land which Jehovah your God gives you, you shall not learn to do after the abominations of those nations. ¹⁰There shall not be found with you any of one that makes his son or his daughter to pass through the fire, one that uses divination, one that practices augury, or an enchanter, or a sorcerer, ¹¹or a charmer, or a consulter with a familiar spirit, or a wizard, or a necromancer. ¹²For whosoever does these things is an abomination unto Jehovah: and because of these abominations Jehovah your God does drive them out from before you. ¹³You shall be perfect with Jehovah your God. ¹⁴For these nations, that you shall dispossess, hearken unto them that practice augury, and unto diviners; but as for you, Jehovah your God has not suffered you so to do.*

In this passage, Moses mentioned eight facets of the occult world:

1. *Divination* means "fortune telling by magical means."
2. *Augury* is soothsaying and trying to determine the future by reading the entrails of animals.
3. An *enchanter* is a magician who puts others under demonic control.
4. A *sorcerer* is one who is involved in witchcraft and astrology.
5. A *charmer* is one who practices magic, miracles, incantations, and hypnotism.
6. A *consulter with a familiar spirit* is a medium who is controlled by a demon. The demon is called "a familiar spirit" probably because he was assigned to the deceased person with whom the medium is trying to communicate. Because this demon had observed the deceased person all of his life and knew all his secrets, he knows how to imitate the deceased person well and is able to pretend that he is the spirit of that dead person.
7. A *wizard* is a clairvoyant or psychic person. The word "wizard" refers to a male witch.
8. A *necromancer* is a medium who consults with the dead.

The second verse to be considered in dealing with the facets of the occult world is Acts 8:9: *But there was a certain man, Simon by name, who beforetime in the city used sorcery, and amazed the people of Samaria, giving out that himself was some great one.* This verse shows that demons are the source of sorcery.

The third verse is Acts 16:16: *And it came to pass, as we were going to the place of prayer, that a certain maid having a spirit of divination met us, who brought her masters much gain by soothsaying.* The Greek word translated as "divination" is *pythōna.* Literally, then, the *spirit of divination* is the spirit of a python. The python is a snake, and in Scripture, the snake is connected with Satan (Gen. 3:1-15; Rev. 12:9; 20:2). So, Satan is the ultimate source of all occultism.

Demons and occultism work hand in hand. In fact, occultism would not exist without demons.

c. The Characteristics of Occultism

Occultism always involves some contact with the demonic world. This is evident from the fact that in every case where occult practice is mentioned, the root word in the Greek harks back to demons. Thus, the various facets of the occult world are all connected with demonic activity.

Occultism involves the uncovering or unveiling of hidden knowledge of the past or future. This is evident from the three Greek words discussed earlier.

Occultism makes promises of extra power. This may be what attracts people to the occult world. It makes promises of mental powers, miracles, and the ability to control other people.

Exodus 20:3-5 states:

> *3You shall have no other gods before me. 4You shall not make unto you a graven image, nor any likeness of anything that is in heaven above, or that is in the earth beneath, or that is in the water under the earth: 5you shall not bow down yourself unto them, nor serve them; for I Jehovah your God am a jealous God, visiting the iniquity of the fathers upon the children, upon the third and upon the fourth generation of them that hate me.*

According to this passage, occultism can lead to the passing on of demonic control to the third and fourth generation. This point is a deduction, because the sin that is passed on to the third and fourth generation is that of the worship of another god. In the context of the above passage, God warned that idolatry and the worship of any other gods would bring punishment, and He would visit the iniquity upon the children and the children's children to the third and the fourth generation. Demons are heavily involved in the area of idolatry and encourage the worship of idols, which is the worship of other gods. Because of the connection between idolatry and demonology, occultism can lead to the passing on of demonic control to the third and the fourth generation.

Occultism requires a meditative or a passive state for demons to operate or take control. This is why activities such as hypnotism, Eastern meditation, and drug abuse are so dangerous.

Occultism creates a strange magnetism that draws the participant while, at the same time, frightens him. People are attracted to it and move into it, but always with some degree of fear and trepidation.

d. The Snares and Practice of Occultism

Satan uses specific traps to ensnare people into the world of the occult and, therefore, also into demonism. There are three categories of traps: spiritism, divination, and magic or sorcery.

(1) Spiritism

In its basic form, spiritism is the consultation with the dead. It can take on five forms. First, there are physical phenomena. This includes levitation, by which the body is lifted; apports, which is the transference of objects from one place to another and moving one solid through another; and telekinesis, which is simple movement of objects without having them move through another solid object.

Second, there are psychic phenomena. This includes visions; automatic writing, which is writing the message of a demon; speaking in a trance; materialization; table lifting; tumbler or glass moving; and excursions of the psyche.

Third, there are metaphysical phenomena. This includes apparitions (meaning visions of a spirit in human form) and ghosts, which are localized in one place, such as a house.

Fourth, there are magic phenomena. This includes magic persecutions (Num. 22:6-7; 24:1), such as the infliction of disease. Balaam was involved in this form of spiritism and was therefore called "Balaam, the soothsayer" in Joshua 13:22. It also includes magic defense whereby one uses incantations to provide protection from magic persecution.

Fifth, there are cultic phenomena. This includes spiritualistic or mystic cults, spiritism proper, and necromancy. Necromancy is a form of spiritism that was prevalent in biblical times and is mentioned in I Samuel 28:3-4; I Chronicles 10:13; and Isaiah 29:4.

(2) *Divination*

In its root meaning, the word "divination" means "the foretelling of the future." Divination is the art of obtaining secret, illegitimate knowledge of the future. There are two different types of divination: artificial and inspirational divination. Artificial divination is also called "augury" and is the practice of reading and interpreting signs and omens. This practice is found in Ezekiel 21:21. Inspirational divination is the receiving of information from a demon speaking through a medium. An example of this is found in Acts 16:16-18.

There are four key words in the Scriptures that refer to those who practice divination: "magicians," "enchanters," "sorcerers" or "soothsayers," and "Chaldeans." All four words are found in the book of Daniel (1:20; 2:2, 10, 27; 4:7; 5:11, 15).

Like spiritism, divination takes on various forms, at least ten of which can be listed:

1. Astrology: This is the most popular form of divination. Its popularity goes back to ancient times. It is mentioned in Deuteronomy 17:2-7; II Kings 23:5; Isaiah 47:12-13; Jeremiah 10:2; Amos 5:25-26; and Acts 7:41-43.

2. Cartomancy: This form of divination uses a deck of cards or Tarot cards for the purpose of foreseeing the future; practitioners of cartomancy are known as "cartomancers" or "card readers."

3. Psychometry: This form of divination is also known as token-object reading and is the alleged ability to discover facts about an event or a person by touching inanimate objects associated with them.

4. Palmistry: This is the practice of interpreting a person's character or predicting his future by examining the person's palms.

5. Divining rod or water witching: In this form of divination, a forked rod is believed to indicate the presence of water by dipping downward when held over a vein.

6. Dowsing: This term describes the use of a pendulum suspended over a map by a thread or a y-shaped metal rod or branch in an attempt to detect hidden substances and even people.

7. Prophetic dreams and visions (Jer. 29:8-9)

8. Ouija: People who practice this form of divination use a board marked with letters, numbers, certain words, and symbols. They take a heart-shaped piece of wood or plastic as a pointer or indicator to spell out messages during a séance.

9. Crystal balls

10. Clairvoyance: This form of divination alleges that one can perceive future things or events. It is an old form of divination, mentioned in Genesis 44:5 and Isaiah 47:9.

(3) *Magic or Sorcery*

Magic or sorcery is the bringing about of certain results beyond man's power through the enlistment of supernatural agencies. It is the actual use of demons to bring about supernatural results.

This snare of occultism has taken on at least thirteen known forms:

1. Black magic: claims to use the forces of evil or Satan

2. White magic: claims to use the forces of good or God (both black and white magic are satanic)

3. Natural magic: claims to use the forces of nature

4. Mental suggestion: transference of thoughts from one mind to another

5. Criminal hypnosis: hypnotizing someone to do something evil

6. Magical mesmerism: healing by touching

7. Healing magic

8. Use of love and hate potions

9. Execration: pronouncement of a specific curse upon someone by the use of a voodoo doll or another object

10. Fertility charms

11. Binding and loosing of Satan: the claim to have the power to do so

12. Death magic

13. Wearing of amulets to ward off bad luck (rather ancient practice found in Gen. 35:4; Judg. 8:21, 26; Isa. 3:18)

e. The Bible and Occultism

The Bible clearly prohibits any contact with the occult. Such prohibitions are found throughout the Scriptures (Ex. 22:18; Lev. 19:26, 31; 20:6, 27; Deut. 18:9-14; I Sam. 15:23; II Kgs. 21:6; Isa. 8:19; Jer. 29:8-9; Mic. 5:12; Acts 19:18-20).

In spite of all of these clear prohibitions, the practice of sorcery was rather popular throughout biblical history (Gen. 41:8; Ex. 7:11; II Kgs. 9:22; 17:17; 23:24; II Chron. 33:6; Isa. 19:3; Jer. 27:9-10; Ez. 21:21; Dan. 1:20; 2:2, 27; 4:7; 5:11; Nah. 3:4; Mal. 3:5; Mt. 7:22-23; Acts 8:9-11; 13:6-11; 19:19; Gal. 5:20; II Tim. 3:8). The Bible records the widespread practice of sorcery, but it clearly forbids believers to have any contact with the occult world.

I. Demonic Control

Sometimes, this area is called "demonic possession," but it will be called "demonic control" in this study for reasons that will be explained below. This division will be discussed in six units: the definition of demonic control, the symptoms of demonic control, the causes of demonic control, the tests of demonic control, the cures of demonic control, and the casting out of demons.

1. The Definition of Demonic Control

In order to arrive at a clear definition of what demonic control means, one must first deal with the key word used in the Scriptures and then with the key expression. In the Greek text, the key word is *daimonizomai*, which means "to be demonized," "to be controlled by a demon from within." This word is frequently translated into English as "possessed by a demon." As was mentioned in previous chapters, the problem with this translation is that the Greek word for "possession" is never used in conjunction with demons. What is found is always *daimonizomai* or "to be controlled by a demon from within." Rather than translating the term as "possessed by a demon," which implies ownership by a demon, it would be far wiser to simply translate it as "controlled by a demon." This key word is found in the Greek text of Matthew 4:24; 8:16, 28, 33; 9:32; 12:22; 15:22; Mark 1:32; 5:15-16, 18; Luke 8:36; and John 10:21.

The Scriptures also present a key expression that means "to have a demon." Examples of the usage of this expression are Matthew 11:18 (*daimonion echei*, meaning literally "a demon he has"); Luke 7:33 (*daimonion echei*); John 7:20 (*daimonion echeis*, meaning literally "a demon you have"); John 8:48 (*daimonion echeis*); John 10:20 (*daimonion echei*); Acts 8:7 (*echontōn pneumata akatharta*, meaning literally "having spirits unclean"); and Acts 16:16 (*echousan pneuma Pythōna*, meaning literally "having a spirit of Python"). The emphasis of the key word is on control, but the emphasis of the key expression is on residence in that the demon is residing within his victim.

By combining the key word and the key expression, a specific definition can be derived:

Demonic control involves a demon residing in a person and exercising direct control over that person with a certain degree of derangement of the mind and/or physical upset of the body.

This definition takes into account the key word, the key expression, and the results. A practical example supporting this definition is found in Matthew 12:43-45, which discusses the demon's place and emphasizes both the key word and the key expression. Mark 5:1-20 gives an example of the result of demonic control, in both the physical and the mental aspects.

To get a clearer picture of what is meant by demonic control, a distinction needs to be made between demonic control and two other types of demonic activities: demonic harassment and demonic influence. Demonic harassment is when a demon plagues a person from without. An example of this is found in Romans 15:22 and I Thessalonians 2:18. These two passages speak of demons hindering the plans of a believer.

An example of demonic influence is found in Matthew 16:21-23:

²¹*From that time began Yeshua to show unto his disciples, that he must go unto Jerusalem, and suffer many things of the elders and*

chief priests and scribes, and be killed, and the third day be raised up. ²²And Peter took him, and began to rebuke him, saying, Be it far from you, Lord: this shall never be unto you. ²³But he turned, and said unto Peter, Get you behind me, Satan: you are a stumbling-block unto me: for you mind not the things of God, but the things of men.

Yeshua's words, "Get you behind me, Satan," show that Peter was under demonic influence. Satan was trying to keep the Messiah from the cross, and he was influencing Peter to accomplish his goal.

Demonic control should be distinguished from both demonic harassment and demonic influence. Demonic harassment and demonic influence are activities outside the person, but demonic control takes place inside the person.

In light of the above definition, can a demon control a believer? Normally, this question is phrased, "Can a believer be possessed by a demon?" As was pointed out earlier, the word "possession" is not a good word to express what one is trying to say because the Greek text never uses that term. If by "possession" one means "ownership," the answer is, "No! A believer can never be possessed by a demon in the sense of ownership." The believer has been purchased by the Messiah according to I Corinthians 6:20. Therefore, he is owned by the Messiah and can never be owned by Satan. But if the question is rephrased according to the biblical usage of the word as "Can a believer be controlled by a demon from within?" then the answer is, "Yes, he can."

There are two passages that make this clear. First is the case of Ananias and Sapphira in Acts 5:1-4:

¹But a certain man named Ananias, with Sapphira his wife, sold a possession, ²and kept back part of the price, his wife also being privy to it, and brought a certain part, and laid it at the apostles' feet. ³But Peter said, Ananias, why has Satan filled your heart to lie to the Holy Spirit, and to keep back part of the price of the land? ⁴While it remained, did it not remain your own? and after it was sold, was it not in your power? How is it that you have conceived this thing in your heart? you have not lied unto men, but unto God.

The Greek word Peter used in verse 3 for "filled" is *eplērōsen*. Paul used the same Greek word in Ephesians 5:18, when he spoke of being *filled with the Spirit*. Just as to be filled with the Spirit means to be controlled by the Holy Spirit, to be filled with Satan means to be controlled by Satan. Since the same Greek word is used, as the Holy Spirit controls from within, so also Satan controls from within. Hence, the Bible does teach that a believer can be controlled by a demon from within.

A second passage is Ephesians 4:27: *neither give place to the devil*. The Greek word Paul used for "place," *topon*, can also mean "beachhead." When an army attacks, it first sends in soldiers to control a beachhead. This beachhead is inside enemy territory. Once the beachhead is secured, reinforcements can come in while those in the beachhead give cover fire. Hence, a beachhead is an area of control within enemy territory. A believer can be controlled through a beachhead within; he can be controlled by a demon.

The distinction between believers and unbelievers is not that the believer cannot be controlled by a demon. Rather, the difference is a matter of the extent of the control. An unbeliever can be totally controlled, but a believer can only be partially controlled.

A common objection to this view is: "How can a demon reside in the same body with the Holy Spirit?" Most believers realize that they have two natures: their old sin nature and their new nature. The Holy Spirit resides in the new nature and coexists with the sin nature of the believer. The demon, on the other hand, does not reside in the new nature, but in the old sin nature. Hence, the fact that there are two natures coexisting within the believer shows how both a demon and the Holy Spirit can coexist within the believer. They simply reside in two different natures.

One last thing by way of definition is that demonic control can be repeated. This is found in Matthew 12:43-45 and Luke 11:24-26.

2. The Symptoms of Demonic Control

How can one tell if someone is controlled by a demon from within? Before dealing with the specific symptoms, a word needs to be said in order to keep one's perspective in balance. The symptoms of demonic control by themselves do not prove that demons are residing in a person. There may be other problems that cause these very same symptoms. There must be a multiplicity of symptoms present to indicate true demonism. This balance must be kept, and one must be careful not to go overboard in one direction or the other. One extreme claims that there is no demonic activity today; the second extreme blames demons for virtually everything. Both extremes must be avoided.

Altogether, there are thirteen symptoms of demonic control. First, demonic control can cause physical disease. This is seen in Matthew 9:32-33. Not all physical maladies are caused by demons. Acts 5:16 distinguishes between people who suffered from ailments because they were demonized and those who were simply afflicted by physical disease, apart from demons.

Second, demonic control can cause mental derangement. This truth is seen in Matthew 17:15. However, again it needs to be pointed out that not all mental derangement is caused by demons. Daniel 4:1-37 records a case of mental illness that was not caused by a demon.

Third, demonic control can cause deep depression. Many people experience normal periods of depression. For example, some respond with depression when they experience failure in business, loss of job, or flunking of a test. Episodes of depression by themselves do not prove demonism. But in the case of depression caused by a demon, one can sense it. One can walk into a room and at once feel a dark cloud of depression, and that is the symptom to which this observation refers.

Fourth, demonic control can cause self-reproach. Demons like to lie to a person, emphasizing the person's lack of self-worth.

Fifth, demons sometimes try to kill the individual in whom they are residing. Therefore, suicidal tendencies and repeated attempts to take one's own life could be a sign that the person is controlled by a demon.

Sixth, demons can cause passivity. Someone who consistently lives in a passive state, who does not seem to be affected by anything that is going on around him, could be controlled by a demon.

Seventh, demons can cause immorality. The Scriptures describe them as "unclean spirits." Characterized by uncleanness, they drive those whom they control to acts of uncleanness (such as premarital sex, adultery, and homosexuality).

Eighth, a constant attitude of bitterness against everything and everybody, against God and the world, can be a symptom of demonic control.

Ninth, often drug abuse and passivity go together. The author has often walked down a busy city street and has seen someone walking toward him who is obviously high on drugs. He was looking, but he did not see; he was totally passive. Drug abuse is often characterized by passivity and can also be a symptom of demonic control.

Tenth, another symptom of demonic control is when people seem to have psychic powers; they seem to know what is going to happen. The author has not dealt with many cases of people under demonic control. In all the years of ministry, there may have been four or five people who very clearly had a demonic problem. One girl was surrounded by a dark cloud of depression, and every time one came into her presence, this cloud was felt. In the case of another girl, she always seemed to know something in advance. She seemed to have unusual psychic abilities and psychic powers. If the doorbell rang, she always knew who it was, even though from where she was sitting or standing, there was no possibility of her knowing who had come to the front door. Psychic power is, indeed, a real symptom of demonic control.

Eleventh, displaying animal-like tendencies can also be a sign of demonic control. In the case of one of the girls mentioned above, she had the ability to devour a whole chicken with her fingers so rapidly that it appeared as if she were a hungry animal. She had animal-like tendencies in her eating habits.

Twelfth, demons can cause restlessness during Bible reading. They do not enjoy hearing the Word of God. It tends to drive them away and to make them agitated. If a person seems quite calm before the Scriptures are opened and then suddenly gets extremely agitated when the Bible is read, this could be a symptom of demonic control.

Thirteenth, when a person displays multiple personalities, it may be a sign of demonic control. Demons have a way of taking on the characteristics of other people. There is often more than one demon residing in a person with multiple personalities. At one point, one demon will speak, and at another point, another demon will speak, thereby causing sudden changes in personalities.

These are thirteen, but not necessarily all, symptoms of demonic control. Again, one must be careful not to become "a demon inspector," assuming people are demonized because they may display a few of these manifestations. There can be other causes for these very same symptoms. Only when there is a multiplicity of signs can one conclude that a person has a demon.

A good example of a person who shows the multiplicity of these symptoms is the Gerasene demoniac, spoken of in Mark 5:1-20. Mark pointed out specific symptoms. There was demonic indwelling in verse 2; unusual physical strength in verse 3; fits of rage in verses 4-5; a split personality in verses 6-7; a resistance to spiritual things in verse 7; excessive sensitivity and sensibility, also in verse 7; alteration of voice in verse 9; and occult transference in verse 13, as the demons moved from the individual into the herd of swine. It was not because the man had one or two of these symptoms, but the fact that he had a multiplicity of symptoms that confirmed he had a demon.

3. The Causes of Demonic Control

From the various passages where demonic elements are described, it is reasonable to deduce that there are four possible causes of demonic control: inheritance, experimentation, transference, and unconfessed sin.

a. Inheritance: Exodus 34:6-7

6And Jehovah passed by before him, and proclaimed, Jehovah, Jehovah, a God merciful and gracious, slow to anger, and abundant in lovingkindness and truth; 7keeping lovingkindness for thousands, forgiving iniquity and transgression and sin; and that will by no means clear the guilty, visiting the iniquity of the fathers upon the children, and upon the children's children, upon the third and upon the fourth generation.

Because Israel was a covenant people, the above was true under the Law of Moses. The particular sin that God visited upon the third and the fourth generation was idolatry and the worship of other gods. If there was some form of idolatry in a person's life, the sin of demonic control could be passed down to the third and fourth generation. Idolatry is not limited to the bowing before statues. Essentially, any form of the occult is a form of idolatry because it involves respect for a god other than the true God. Hence, behind idolatry is the aspect of demonism. It needs to be understood that the Mosaic Law does not operate today. It is not the rule of life for the believer, nor can it be used to try to develop spiritual principles to avoid demonic control or the need for deliverance. It has become a fad in certain movements of the Christian church to claim that one needs to break generational bondage, but that is simply not biblically valid.

To begin with, the Mosaic Law, with its principle of God visiting the sins of the fathers down to the fourth generation, was true only in reference to Israel because of Israel's covenantal relationship. It does not apply to the Gentiles nor to the church today. Furthermore, once a person receives the Lord, he is regenerated and any bondage to sin is broken immediately. One does not need to go around renouncing previous generational sins. This is just a fad that has permeated segments of the evangelical church, and certain teachers have misused the Scriptures in trying to hold to this premise. While the consequences of idolatry were true for Israel under the Mosaic Law, they did not apply to Gentiles during the same time period, nor are they true for believers today. When we are regenerated, we are saved completely, and that includes salvation from any generational sin.

Spiritual problems are easily solved when people conform themselves to the spiritual principles of the Law of the Messiah, and there is no need to try to explain them by claiming that the Mosaic Law somehow still applies today. It does not now and never did apply to Gentiles.

People often pray the way they have been taught and often follow the newest gimmicks, such as "binding the spirits." As the Holy Spirit does not violate His own Word, people are not led by the Spirit to pray against generational sins. Whatever the Holy Spirit does by way of leading people today would be consistent with the written Word of God. All of the prayers of the apostles and the principles of the New Testament, while dealing with the issues of sins in various believers' lives, never mention praying to break any generational bondage. People have simply taken a principle out of a law that applied exclusively to Israel as a covenantal people and have applied it to believers today. By so doing, they have devalued the accomplishments of the blood of Messiah on the cross—an act that brings instantaneous deliverance from any bondage of sin to the one who believes.

The proper way of handling sin in the believer's life is the way of Romans 6. According to this passage, we must recognize that both our sin nature and our *old man* were co-crucified with the Messiah the moment we believed, thus breaking the bondage to sin. Now we must make the decision not to let our bodies be used as instruments for sin. This is the New Testament pattern believers should follow.

b. Experimentation: I Corinthians 10:14-22

14Wherefore, my beloved, flee from idolatry. 15I speak as to wise men; judge ye what I say. 16The cup of blessing which we bless, is it not a communion of the blood of Messiah? The bread which we break, is it not a communion of the body of Messiah? 17seeing that we, who are many, are one bread, one body: for we all partake of the one bread. 18Behold Israel after the flesh: have not they that eat the sacrifices communion with the altar? 19What say I then? that a thing sacrificed to idols is anything, or that an idol is anything? 20But I say, that the things which the Gentiles sacrifice, they sacrifice to demons, and not to God: and I would not that ye should have communion with demons. 21Ye cannot drink the cup of the Lord, and the cup of demons: ye cannot partake of the table of the Lord, and of the table of demons. 22Or do we provoke the Lord to jealousy? are we stronger than he?

Some people experiment with the occult and fall under demonic control as a result. God has forbidden any contact with the occult world, which is under demonic control. This prohibition must be strictly obeyed.

c. Transference: Mark 5:9-13

9And he [Yeshua] asked him, What is your name? And he says unto him, My name is Legion; for we are many. 10And he besought him much that he would not send them away out of the country. 11Now there was there on the mountain side a great herd of swine feeding. 12And they besought him, saying, Send us into the swine, that we may enter into them. 13And he gave them leave. And the unclean spirits came out, and entered into the swine: and the herd rushed down the steep into the sea, in number about two thousand; and they were drowned in the sea.

Even when one has never directly practiced the occult, simply having contact with it by observing it or merely being present as it is practiced can result in demonic transference. Because of this transference, there is demonic control.

d. Unconfessed Sin: Ephesians 4:27

In Ephesians 4:27, Paul wrote: *neither give place to the devil*. It is possible for a believer to be under demonic control from within. In this verse, believers are warned against giving a beachhead to the devil. As discussed earlier, a beachhead is always an area of control within enemy territory, not from the outside. The context of this verse is that of unconfessed sin, and the implication is that the means by which some have fallen under demonic control is by unconfessed sin.

4. The Tests for Demonic Control

It was previously mentioned that one can make certain deductions about a person's spiritual condition when he displays several symptoms of demonic control. However, there is the additional aspect of testing the spirits, because the display of certain symptoms by itself does not prove that demonic control is being exercised.

That believers should test the spirits is taught in I John 4:1: *Beloved, believe not every spirit, but prove the spirits, whether they are of God; because many false prophets are gone out into the world.*

There are three specific tests and three specific questions that one can ask to see if someone or something is of the Lord or of a demon. The first test is based on I John 4:2-4 and addresses the incarnation:

²Hereby know ye the Spirit of God: every spirit that confesses that Yeshua Messiah is come in the flesh is of God: ³and every spirit that confesses not Yeshua is not of God: and this is the spirit of the antichrist, whereof ye have heard that it comes; and now it is in the world already. ⁴Ye are of God, my little children, and have overcome them: because greater is he that is in you than he that is in the world.

In testing a spirit, a helpful question is this: "Has the Messiah come in the flesh?" or asked differently, "Did God become man in the person of Yeshua of Nazareth?" Verse 2 makes it clear that demons will deny the incarnation. Hence, if we ask someone this question and do not get a positive answer, then the person we asked has failed the test. The failure may imply that there is a demon involved.

The second test pertains to the Lordship of Messiah. The basis for this test is I Corinthians 12:3: *Wherefore I make known unto you, that no man speaking in the Spirit of God says, Yeshua is anathema; and no man can say, Yeshua is Lord, but in the Holy Spirit.* This verse allows for another question that may be asked: "Is Yeshua the Messiah Lord?" In this case, the term "Lord" does not refer to a master who happens to own slaves. Rather, it refers to "Lord" in the sense of the Jehovah of the Hebrew Scriptures. So, the question is whether Yeshua is the Messiah Lord, meaning the *YHWH* of the Old Testament. If there is a denial of the lordship of the Messiah, then one can suspect a demon because the second test has also been failed.

The third test pertains to the blood of the Messiah. It is based on I John 5:6-7: *This is he that came by water and blood, even Yeshua Messiah; not with the water only, but with the water and with the blood. And it is the Spirit that bears witness, because the Spirit is the truth.* If the person reacts negatively to the mention of the blood of the Messiah, he has failed the third test, and it may be an indication of demonic problems.

These three questions can be used to test the spirits. If the person denies the incarnation, denies the lordship of the Messiah, and reacts negatively to the mentioning of Messiah's blood, there is a strong indication that demons are involved. However, these tests must be applied only when it is apparent that the demon is exercising control; otherwise, it will not work. Even when a person has a demon in him, the demon may be laying low. At that moment, he might not be exercising direct control; he might be "benign." In other words, the demon is still in the person, but it is the person himself who is in control. If one were to apply the three tests at that very moment, the person would pass the tests. One needs to wait until the demon is in control, as determined by the symptoms discussed earlier, and then apply these tests. Failing the tests may be a good indication that demons are involved.

5. The Cures for Demonic Control

Five things will be mentioned briefly in answer to the question whether there are any cures for demonic control. These points will be expanded in the next main section dealing with demonism and the believer.

The first cure is in relation to the unbeliever. This cure is receiving the Messiah. The unbeliever needs to believe the gospel as defined in I Corinthians 15:1-4 and that Yeshua is his Savior and accept Him as such.

The second cure is in relation to the believer. This cure is confession of sin. As was mentioned previously, some believers fall under demonic control because of unconfessed sin.

A third cure is the prayer of renunciation. As a reminder, demonic control that was inherited prior to salvation is broken once and for all at conversion. The believer is freed from the authority of Satan the moment he is saved. In such cases, a prayer of renunciation is not necessary. The prayer of renunciation would only be necessary in those situations in which a believer has backslidden and gotten himself involved in occultism and has fallen under some element of control. As for all other sins, believers must confess these sins to be restored to fellowship. Renunciation of control would be part of that confession in this particular case.

A fourth cure is that there should be the removal of all occult objects. An example of such an action is seen in Acts 19:19: *And not a few of them that practised magical arts brought their books together and burned them in the sight of all; and they counted the price of them, and found it fifty thousand pieces of silver.* If one has any occult objects in the home, such as Ouija boards, they should be removed.

A fifth cure is resistance. This cure is found in James 4:7: *resist the devil so that he will flee.*

6. The Casting Out of Demons

The ultimate cure for demonic control is exorcism, that is, the casting out of a demon. The fact that demons can be exorcised is clearly taught in Scripture by many examples. One example is that of the Messiah. In the Gospel of Mark alone, we read of Yeshua casting out demons in 1:23-27, 32-34, 39; 3:11-12; 5:1-20; 7:25-30; and 9:17-29. The twelve apostles also cast out demons (Mt. 10:1; Mk. 3:14-15), and so did the seventy disciples (Lk. 10:17). The Gospels record other believers who, although they were not always following Yeshua around the land, still cast out demons (Mk. 9:38-39; Lk. 9:49-50). Peter cast out demons in Acts 5:16; Philip in Acts 8:7; and Paul in Acts 16:16-18 and 19:11-12. All of these examples show that demons who reside in people can be cast out.

Altogether, there are five ways exorcism can be performed. The first means is that demons are cast out in the name of Yeshua the Messiah. This is seen in Luke 10:17: *And the seventy returned with joy, saying, Lord, even the demons are subject unto us in your name.*

The second means is by the power of the Holy Spirit. One should not cast out demons in his own name, but in the name of the Messiah; it must not be by one's own power, but by the power of the Holy Spirit. This is found in Matthew 12:28, where Yeshua said, *But if I by the Spirit of God cast out demons, then is the kingdom of God come upon you.*

The third means is with a simple word, that is, with a command, as in Matthew 8:16: *And when even was come, they brought unto him many possessed with demons: and he cast out the spirits with a word, and healed all that were sick* (cf. Mk. 5:8). There is no need to go through a long ritual to cast out a demon. It should be sufficient to simply command the demon out with a word, and that word is, "Get out in the name of Yeshua the Messiah."

The fourth means is faith. This is found in Matthew 17:18-20:

[18]And Yeshua rebuked him; and the demon went out of him: and the boy was cured from that hour. [19] Then came the disciples to Yeshua apart, and said, Why could not we cast it out? [20]And he said unto them, Because of your little faith: for verily I say unto you, If ye have faith as a grain of mustard seed, ye shall say unto this mountain,

Remove hence to yonder place; and it shall remove; and nothing shall be impossible unto you.

The believer must believe that he has the power and authority through the Messiah to cast out demons.

Fifth, while some demons can simply be ordered out in the name of the Messiah, by the power of the Spirit, with a word, and on the basis of faith, there are certain types of demons that cannot be removed by these means. For example, a demon that causes a person to be mute needs to be prayed out. This is found in Mark 9:29: *And he said unto them, This kind can come out by nothing, save by prayer.* In such cases, one does not try to get a demon out by using the authority of the name of the Messiah. Rather, God will accomplish it by means of the prayers of the saints.

As pointed out earlier, both believers and unbelievers can be controlled by a demon. In the case of an unbeliever, a believer must force the demon out by ordering him to leave in the name of the Messiah, in the power of the Spirit, on the basis of faith, and in certain situations by prayer. The believer must do it, because the unbeliever has no spiritual authority whatsoever to do it for himself.

However, in the case of a believer who is controlled by a demon, this is not the best course of action. As mentioned earlier, the difference between believers and unbelievers is that the unbeliever can be totally controlled, but a believer can only be partially controlled by a demon. There is always a part of him consistently under God's control. Because one is a believer, it is not necessary to have another believer force the demon out; the believer can force the demon out himself. That is why, in dealing with Satan, the believer is encouraged to do one thing: to resist (Jas. 4:7; I Pet. 5:8-9; Eph. 6:10-18). Believers are instructed to resist Satan a total of five times in these three passages. If a believer resists Satan, he can force the demon out of himself.

The means of resisting Satan is given in Ephesians 6:10: *be strong in the Lord.* The way to be strong in the Lord is to put on the whole armor of God. To put on the whole armor means to understand the believer's position in Messiah, to understand positional truth. Because of what believers are positionally in Messiah, having been baptized into His body, they have spiritual authority. The trouble is that believers do not always know the spiritual authority they have, and so they fail to exercise it. Believers must learn of their position in Messiah and the spiritual authority that comes with it.[14]

J. Demonism and the Believer

There are four points that explain how demonism relates to the believer. First, demons oppose the saints on a continuous basis. This form of opposition can take on several forms:

- There is general opposition, which sometimes comes through as direct opposition from demons. This is seen in Ephesians 6:12: *For our wrestling is not against flesh and blood, but against the principalities, against the powers, against the world-rulers of this darkness, against the spiritual hosts of wickedness in the heavenly places.*

- There is also demonic opposition to believers through unbelievers, as seen in Ephesians 2:2: *wherein ye once walked according to the course of this world, according to the prince of the powers of the air, of the spirit that now works in the sons of disobedience.*

- Furthermore, there is opposition against specific individual believers, as seen in Ephesians 2:3: *among whom we also all once lived in the lusts of our flesh, doing the desires of the flesh and of the mind, and were by nature children of wrath, even as the rest.*

- Lastly, there is opposition to a body of believers, a local church. This can be seen in Revelation 2:24: *But to you I say, to the rest that are in Thyatira, as many as have not this teaching, who know not the deep things of Satan, as they are wont to say; I cast upon you none other burden.*

Second, God uses demons for the spiritual growth of believers. He will allow some degree of demonic activity from without—not from within—to mature His children. For example, in II Corinthians 12:7 God

---

[14] For a study of the believer's position in Messiah, we recommend Messianic Bible Study #110, "Thirty-Three Things: A Study of Positional Truth," available at https://www.ariel.org/.

used a demon to teach Paul humility: *And by reason of the exceeding greatness of the revelations, that I should not be exalted overmuch, there was given to me a thorn in the flesh, a messenger of Satan to buffet me, that I should not be exalted overmuch.*

Third, demons were defeated at the cross. This point is made in Colossians 2:15: *having despoiled the principalities and the powers, he made a show of them openly, triumphing over them in it.* This means that demons have no legal authority over a believer unless he willingly submits to them. Believers obey demons only if they allow themselves to fall into one of those demonic traps listed earlier.

Fourth, believers have responsibilities in the context of demonism. As was pointed out earlier, I John 4:1-4 teaches that a believer should learn how to test the spirits. There should be no consultation and no connection with the occult (Lev. 19:31; Deut. 18:9-14; Isa. 8:19). In I Corinthians 10:20, Paul warned that there should be no fellowship with those connected with demonic activity: *But I say, that the things which the Gentiles sacrifice, they sacrifice to demons, and not to God: and I would not that ye should have communion with demons.* Finally, Ephesians 6:10-18 states that believers should wear the whole armor of God, which is the Scriptures.

K. The Future Activities of Demons

The future activities of demons can be divided into two categories: what they have been doing and will do in the last days of the church age and what they will do during the tribulation.

During the last days, demons will spread false doctrine in the church to bring about the great apostasy. This has already been fulfilled over the course of the 20th century. The majority of the visible church today has gone apostate. This was predicted as a future activity of demons in I Timothy 4:1-3:

¹But the Spirit says expressly, that in later times some shall fall away from the faith, giving heed to seducing spirits and doctrines of demons, ² through the hypocrisy of men that speak lies, branded in their own conscience as with a hot iron; ³forbidding to marry, and commanding to abstain from meats, which God created to be received with thanksgiving by them that believe and know the truth.

During the tribulation, there will be a tremendous increase in demonic activity, as it was in the days of the Gospels. There will be at least four specific activities performed by demons during the tribulation.

First, Revelation 9 states that there will be two demonic invasions during this seven-year period. The first demonic invasion will be for the purpose of tormenting men greatly, short of death, for five months (vv. 1-11). The second demonic invasion will be for the purpose of destroying one-third of humanity (vv. 15-19). This invasion will be spearheaded by the four leading demons who are currently bound at the Euphrates River in Iraq (vv. 14-15). They will lead a total of two hundred million demons who will be released out of the abyss for this purpose.

Second, Revelation 9:20-21 reveals the fact that during the tribulation, men will begin to worship demons on a scale greater than ever seen in human history.

Third, along with Satan, demons will be cast out of their present abode, the atmospheric heavens. According to Revelation 12:7-12, they will be confined to the earth for the second half of the tribulation. This explains why there will be such a tremendous increase in demonic activity during this time.

The fourth specific activity is that demons will help gather the nations for that final war, the Campaign of Armageddon. Revelation 16:13-14 speaks of demons with frog-like characteristics going forth to make sure that nations come together for that final conflict.

L. The Doom of Demons

The doom of demons will come in two stages: during the millennium and during the eternal order.

As to the millennium, demons will be in a place of confinement during Messiah's thousand-year reign on earth. This is the point of Isaiah 24:21-22, which states that God is going to punish the *high ones on high*—the fallen angelic beings who will be put into prison. All demons will be confined during the entire millennium, so there will be no demonic activity whatsoever in the Messianic kingdom.

Many assume that the demons will be confined with Satan in the abyss, but that is not what the Bible teaches. Satan himself will be confined in the abyss. The demons, however, will be divided into two groups and confined in two places. The first group will be confined in the land of Edom, which today is the southern part of Jordan. This is the point of Isaiah 34:13-15:

> *13And thorns shall come up in its palaces, nettles and thistles in the fortresses thereof; and it shall be a habitation of jackals, a court for ostriches. 14And the wild beasts of the desert shall meet with the wolves, and the wild goat shall cry to his fellow; yea, the night-monster shall settle there, and shall find her a place of rest. 15There shall the dart-snake make her nest, and lay, and hatch, and gather under her shade; yea, there shall the kites be gathered, every one with her mate.*

This passage mentions various animals living in a land of burning pitch and burning brimstone. But we know that literal animals like those mentioned cannot live in such a land, so these beings with particular animal-like features are demons. The Hebrew term for "wild goat" refers to demons in goat form. The Hebrew term for "night monster" refers to night demons, those who are active at night hours.

The second group of demons will be confined in the city of Babylon, located within modern-day Iraq. This is the point of Isaiah 13:21-22 and Revelation 18:2:

✧ Isaiah 13:21-22: *21But wild beasts of the desert shall lie there; and their houses shall be full of doleful creatures; and ostriches shall dwell there, and wild goats*[15] *shall dance there. 22And wolves shall cry in their castles, and jackals in the pleasant palaces: and her time is near to come, and her days shall not be prolonged.*

✧ Revelation 18:2: *And he cried with a mighty voice, saying, Fallen, fallen is Babylon the great, and is become a habitation of demons,*

---

[15] The mention of "wild goats" again makes it clear that these are demons.

and a hold of every unclean spirit, and a hold of every unclean and hateful bird.

Because demons will be confined in Edom and Babylon, these two regions of the world will be areas of desolation throughout the kingdom period and will be places of burning pitch and burning brimstone, with the smoke of the brimstone ascending for the entire millennium. So, while the whole world is beautified and blossoming as a rose, these two areas will be desolate. No humans will live there, only the demons who are confined there.

There will be no demonic activity of any kind—no harassment, influence, or control—throughout the Messianic kingdom. Whatever sin is found during this time will be the result of man's sin nature rather than demonic activity.

The second stage of the doom of demons will come in the eternal order, and it will come in two phases. First, every demon will be judged at the Great White Throne Judgment by believers. In I Corinthians 6:3, Paul stated that someday believers will judge the angels. He did not mean good angels, because holy angels never sin and never fail in their missions. The angels to be judged are fallen angels or demons. The Great White Throne Judgment will determine their individual degree of punishment. Not all demons have the same degree of wickedness, so there will be degrees of punishment even for demons. That degree will be determined by believers.

Second, after the Great White Throne Judgment, demons will be cast into the lake of fire, where they will spend eternity (Mt. 8:29; 25:41). This will be the final doom of demons.

M. Questions and Study Suggestions

Study Suggestion 1: Write the letter of the definition next to the correct corresponding name.

1. (___) angels of evil

a. "to rule"; it pictures demons lording it over others

2. (___) ĕlîlim

b. "rūaḥ rā'āh"; emphasizes the very nature of demons

3. (___) evil spirit

c. "night demon"

4. (___) familiar spirit

d. Psalm 78:49, literally (some translations read "destroying angels")

5. (___) gāḏ

e. demons of "fate"

6. (___) qeṭeḇ

f. "fortune"; demons that have some control over destiny and future

7. (___) lîlîṯ

g. demons of "destruction"; found in Ps. 91:6

8. (___) lying spirit

h. These demons can impersonate a departed loved one at a séance.

9. (___) meni

i. This term may refer to holy angels or fallen angels, because God created them all.

10. (___) śə'îrim

j. Demons in goat form; the church of Satan uses a goat head as its satanic symbol because of the appearance of these demons.

11. (___) šêḏîm

k. The influence of demons is behind idolatry.

12. (___) sons of God

l. Demons do not tell the truth.

Study Suggestion 2: Look up the following Scripture references and write the demonic titles that indicate some kind of rank.

I Corinthians 15:24

　　a. _____

　　b. _____

　　c. _____

Ephesians 6:12

    a. _____

    b. _____

    c. _____

    d. Which of the above terms is a translation of the Greek word for "cosmocrats"?

Colossians 2:15

    a. _____

    b. _____

Fill in the blanks:

1. There is consistent, continuous demonic opposition to the saints, which takes three forms:

    a. General opposition, which can be either _____ or _____.

    b. Opposition against _____

    c. _____ opposition, particularly against (what type?) _____

2. In spite of everything listed in the previous point, God sometimes uses demons for a good purpose: the _____ of believers.

3. According to Colossians 2:15, the principalities and powers were despoiled; the demons were decisively defeated at the cross. However, you have just studied that demons are immensely busy with evil activities; so, in what sense were they "defeated"?

4. To determine whether or not something is demonic, believers must _____ the _____.

5. A believer should have no personal _____ with the occult world.

6. A believer should not _____ with anyone connected with demonic activity.

7. Believers must *put on the whole armor of God*, which entails _____ and _____ upon the Scriptures. Next to each phrase below, write either the word "purpose" or "benefit" to tell whether it is a direct purpose of, or a benefit derived from, putting on the armor of God:

    a. _____ – To become more holy and devoted to God

    b. _____ – To know how to deal with specific situations biblically

c. _____ – To become more knowledgeable

d. _____ – To spend more quality time with God

e. _____ – To be able to use the Scriptures effectively in daily life

f. _____ – To resist Satan

Answer these questions:

1. Can a believer cast out a demon from himself or herself?
2. Can a believer cast out a demon from another believer?
3. Can a believer cast out a demon from an unbeliever?
4. Can an unbeliever cast out a demon from himself?

CPSIA information can be obtained
at www.ICGtesting.com
Printed in the USA
BVHW042105030121
596006BV00008B/18